MILITARY OPERATIONS FROM KOSOVO TO KABUL

To Henry

MILITARY OPERATIONS FROM KOSOVO TO KABUL

THE UNIQUE EXPERIENCES OF A COMBAT LAWYER

COLONEL JAMES NELSON

Pen & Sword
MILITARY

AN IMPRINT OF PEN & SWORD BOOKS LTD.
YORKSHIRE – PHILADELPHIA

First published in Great Britain in 2021 by
PEN AND SWORD MILITARY
An imprint of
Pen & Sword Books Ltd
Yorkshire – Philadelphia

Copyright © Colonel James Nelson, 2021

ISBN 978 1 39900 461 9

The right of Colonel James Nelson to be identified as Author of this work has been asserted by him in accordance with the Copyright, Designs and Patents Act 1988.

A CIP catalogue record for this book is available from the British Library.

All rights reserved. No part of this book may be reproduced or transmitted in any form or by any means, electronic or mechanical including photocopying, recording or by any information storage and retrieval system, without permission from the Publisher in writing.

Typeset in Times New Roman 11.5/14 by
SJmagic DESIGN SERVICES, India.
Printed and bound by CPI Group (UK) Ltd, Croydon, CR0 4YY

Pen & Sword Books Limited incorporates the imprints of Atlas, Archaeology, Aviation, Discovery, Family History, Fiction, History, Maritime, Military, Military Classics, Politics, Select, Transport, True Crime, Air World, Frontline Publishing, Leo Cooper, Remember When, Seaforth Publishing, The Praetorian Press, Wharncliffe Local History, Wharncliffe Transport, Wharncliffe True Crime and White Owl.

For a complete list of Pen & Sword titles please contact
PEN & SWORD BOOKS LIMITED
47 Church Street, Barnsley, South Yorkshire, S70 2AS, England
E-mail: enquiries@pen-and-sword.co.uk
Website: www.pen-and-sword.co.uk

Or
PEN AND SWORD BOOKS
1950 Lawrence Rd, Havertown, PA 19083, USA
E-mail: Uspen-and-sword@casematepublishers.com
Website: www.penandswordbooks.com

Contents

Acknowledgements		vi
Abbreviations and Acronyms		viii
Foreword *by Sir Julian Brazier, TD*		xi
Introduction		xiii
Chapter 1	On Her Majesty's Legal Service	1
Chapter 2	*Audentis Fortuna Iuvat*	19
Chapter 3	The Front-line Factory	42
Chapter 4	The Lord Chief Justice of Kosovo	63
Chapter 5	ARRC Revisited	78
Chapter 6	Welcome to Kabul	91
Chapter 7	Kill or Capture	111
Chapter 8	Hearts and Minds	134
Epilogue	*Justitia in Armis*	142
Notes		145

Acknowledgements

First, to my wife and son, for their unfailing support and secondly, to Sir Julian Brazier for kindly agreeing to provide the foreword.

I have long since lost contact with the officers and men of 2/7 Gurkha Rifles but my brief experience of life with them in the Far East kindled my interest in the army and stood me in very good stead during my later military career, as well as providing the background to this book. For me, Brunei established the benchmark for discomfort on military duty – even though we were only on exercise! – and I am full of admiration for those men and their successors in our, now sadly much diminished, Brigade of Gurkhas.

Both on and off operations, my friends and colleagues in the ALC/ALS have not only always been professionally supportive and a tremendous help – and great company socially – but also an inspiration for this book, which I hope illustrates the importance as well as some of the challenges and frustrations of operational law.

Among them, in no particular order, my special thanks go to John Taylor, Mike Clarke, David Hawley, Tom Glynn, Neil Jones, Roger Lewis, Stephen Vowles, Jeremy Moon, Charles Swabey, Gordon Risius, Phil McEvoy, Patrick Mason, John Bowman, Jane Eyton-Jones, Alasdair Morrison, John Hardy, Gary Adams, Darren Stewart, Charles Bullough, Cathy Braddick-Hughes, David Reddin, Philip Norris, Pippa Hanson, Tony Paphiti, Jo Bowen, Nigel and Juliet Jones, Mark Dakers, Charlie and Leigh Barnett, Jim Johnston, Gavin Davies, Mike Cole, Dick Austin, Tim Matthews, Dieter Rollecke, Lee Burney, Neil Keery and Anna Labus, and now sadly deceased John Murray, Mike Fugard and Tony Rogers.

I have worked with many others in various organizations, both preparing and deploying on these operations whom I would like to thank for their help, encouragement and companionship. In particular, Generals Mike Jackson, Andrew Ridgway and Mike Maples in the ARRC first

Acknowledgements

time round and Richard Shirreff, Tim Evans and Curtis Scaparotti, as well as Iain Harrison, Paddy Allison, Mark Wentworth, Mike Bennett, Martin Lilley, Rob Davie, Pat Cairns, Sally Finch and Pietro d'Andrea the second time.

Also, thanks to my Dutch legal colleagues, Wiebe Baron and Bart Haverman and roommate René Pals.

In the US JAG Corps: in Kosovo, thanks to Brian Palmer and Mark Martins, and in Kabul to all the crew in the 'Swamp' at KAIA, brilliantly led by Walt 'Rock' Hudson, not forgetting Dave Swanson the Aussie. I worked closely with US officers during my operational deployments and, contrary to the impression which may be given by many of my old-fashioned references to the way they sometimes do business, I found them tremendous comrades.

Thank you to all the permanent and visiting staff and presenters at the International Institute for Humanitarian Law in San Remo, Italy, especially my friends, Juhani Loikannen, Karl Edlinger, Maria Jonsson, Patrizia di Pietro and the late André Retief.

Also, to all those at the 'sharp end'. With sincere apologies to the many failed by my geriatric memory.

This book is for my dear brother Henry Stuart Stythe, who died of Covid-19 while I was writing it.

Abbreviations and Acronyms

AFOR	Albania Force
AFSouth	Armed Forces South
ALA	Army Legal Aid – later Army Legal Assistance
ALC	Army Legal Corps
ALS	Army Legal Services
ANA	Afghan National Army
ANSF	Afghan National Security Forces
AP(s)	Additional Protocol(s) to the GCs
APA	Army Prosecuting Authority
CAP	combat air patrol
CDS	Chief of Defence Staff
CG	Commanding General
COIN	counterinsurgency
COS	Chief of Staff
CP	close protection
CSBM	Confidence and Security Building Measures
DFac	dining facility
DOT	Detention Oversight Team
DPH	directly participating in hostilities
ECHR	European Convention on Human Rights
ECSC	European Coal and Steel Community
FARC	Fuerzas Armadas Revolutionarios de Colombia
FOB	forward operating base
FRY	Federal Republic of Yugoslavia
FYROM	Former Yugoslav Republic of Macedonia
GCs	Geneva Convention(s)
HQNI	Headquarters Northern Ireland
IAC	international armed conflict
ICTY	International Criminal Tribunal for Yugoslavia
IHL	International Humanitarian Law

Abbreviations and Acronyms

IED	improvised explosive device
IMP	International Military Police
ISAF	International Security Assistance Force
IJC	ISAF Joint Command
ICRC	International Committee of the Red Cross
INLA	Irish National Liberation Army
JAG Corps	Judge Advocate General's Corps
JIAT	Joint Incident Assessment Team
JOC	joint operations centre
KAIA	Kabul International Airport
KFOR	Kosovo Force
KLA	Kosovo Liberation Army
LOAC	law of armed conflict
MEJA	Military Extra-territorial Jurisdiction Act
MOAG	member of an armed group
MTA	Military Technical Agreement
NAC	North Atlantic Council
NATO	North Atlantic Treaty Organization
NDS	National Directorate of Security
NGO	non-governmental organization
NIAC	non-international armed conflict
NORAid	Northern Irish Aid Committee
OSCE	Organization for Security and Cooperation in Europe
PfP	Partnership for Peace
PIRA	Provisional Irish Republican Army
PJHQ	Permanent Joint Headquarters
PLA	People's Liberation Army
PRT	Provincial Reconstruction Team
PX	post exchange
QED	*quod erat demonstrandum*
QGO	Queen's Gurkha Officer
RCB	Regular Commissions Board
RMAS	Royal Military Academy Sandhurst
ROE	rules of engagement
RSC	Rear Support Command
SFOR	Stabilization Force
SHAPE	Supreme Headquarters Allied Powers Europe
SNR	senior national representative

SOFA	Status of Forces Agreement
SRSG	Special Representative of the Secretary-General
UAV	unmanned aerial vehicle
UNAMA	United Nations Assistance Mission Afghanistan
UNSCR	United Nations Security Council Resolution
UNMIK	United Nations Mission in Kosovo
USAID	United States Agency for International Development
WAAF	Women's Auxiliary Air Force
WO	Warrant Officer

Foreword

By Sir Julian Brazier, TD

I am delighted to have the opportunity to write this foreword for James Nelson's unusual and highly readable perspective on a range of British military operations. In recent times, legal issues affecting our servicemen and -women have become more and more prominent in the media, both regarding overseas operations in Iraq and Afghanistan and, more recently, the controversial emergence of court cases against elderly veterans of the Northern Ireland troubles.

James's service as a legal officer in a range of different theatres, including Northern Ireland, Kosovo and Afghanistan, gives him a fascinating perspective on the challenges our soldiers face. He brings to the table a combination of a lucid legal mind and a clear understanding – and sympathy for – the men and women risking their lives on our behalf, which started with his gap-year commission with the Gurkhas in Brunei and Hong Kong.

James wears his learning lightly, writing with an engaging and colourful style. He explains candidly why the intervention in Kosovo was illegal, before outlining the measures he and his colleagues took to help ensure that the soldiers on the ground operated within the international law of armed conflict, even though their political masters had driven a coach and horses through it (perhaps for good reason – his account is remarkably balanced). Most readers will be surprised to hear that our troops were deployed to our rather unwilling allies in Macedonia with no more legal 'top cover' than tourists.

The text is sprinkled with wider observations – I was intrigued to hear that President Karzai 'was allegedly rather too fond of some of his country's unusual agricultural products'. James illustrates how the interface between public relations and international law has a profound effect on military decision-making, pointing out that, by the latter stages of the ISAF campaign, NATO was planning its missions on the basis of requiring zero civilian casualties, making operations against a ruthless foe extremely difficult. Yet he balances the questions that he poses with a fascinating account of the centrality of the Rule of Law in reconstructing the Colombian armed forces' approach to dealing with the FARC, in which he played a role.

Throughout, James's style is self-deprecating with quiet humour. We are with him in the shelter in what appears to be shelling and turns out to be an earthquake and in the uncovering of misdemeanours, from Scandinavians stealing precious water for illicit swimming pools to Afghans stealing petrol – the latter with truly tragic consequences.

This is a fascinating account of a life of service close to, and occasionally at the sharp end of, operations, and woven in and out of the centres of power and decision-making. Anyone interested in how decisions are made in military campaigns, or with a wider interest in Britain's military adventures abroad, should read and enjoy it.

Julian Brazier

Introduction

On the evening of 9 November 1989, I had just bought a round of drinks[1] in the officers' mess, Old College, at the Royal Military Academy, Sandhurst (RMAS) when one of my colleagues came downstairs from watching the news to announce to the somewhat incredulous assembled company that the Berlin wall had fallen.

This event marked the beginning of the end of the Cold War, which, although it turned out to be what some would call a 'phoney war', had been arguably the most perilous half-century in human history, with the ever-present threat of mutually assured nuclear destruction hanging over the world. Indeed, the war's true end which followed a couple of years later was famously referred to as 'the end of history',[2] the endpoint of mankind's ideological evolution and the universalization of Western liberal democracy as the final form of human government. Those conclusions may have since proved to be somewhat premature but for the time being at least, the 'Triumph of the West' seemed assured. The fact that this was achieved peacefully was largely attributable to two seemingly unrelated weapons in the western armoury.

First, the conclusion of the Second World War marked the inception throughout Western Europe of rules-based government. That is not to suggest that before that time most countries were in a state of anarchy, but as the neighbouring nations huddled ever closer together politically and commercially, a number of treaty obligations, from the Geneva Conventions (GC) of 1949 and the European Convention of Human Rights (ECHR) the following year to the beginnings of the Common Market with the ECSC the year after that, confirmed the rule of law as the universal norm. This legal construct lent tremendous confidence, stability and legitimacy to the fight to restrain the ideological threat from the East.

Secondly there was NATO, itself the offspring of a Treaty[3] (there is a clue in the name), formed again in the aftermath of the Nazi scare specifically to provide the politico-military 'big stick' which was rightly seen as essential to curtail the Soviet bogeyman. But as recent history has taught us, and as I experienced myself in years to come, the end of the Cold War was far from the end of NATO.

The GCs include a requirement for the Law of Armed Conflict (LOAC) to be 'disseminated widely'[4] and those Conventions were themselves supplemented by two Additional Protocols (APs) in 1977, the first of which makes specific provision for armed forces to include legal advisers.[5] In fact, the one-time Director General of UK Army Legal Services, Major-General Mike Conway, was fond of teasing his lay contemporary officers that legal officers were the only soldiers who were legally required on the battlefield and the remainder were just 'nice to have'.

In order to fulfil that requirement, as well as to provide the expertise necessary to advise them on other legal matters such as military discipline, the armed forces of any nation need from time to time to instruct legal advisers. In many cases this is achieved by recruiting lawyers into the armed forces as serving officers, in exactly the same way as doctors are recruited as medical officers.

It was this requirement which gave birth to the Army Legal Corps, and when I joined in 1982 the British regular army, numbering something in the region of 130,000 included about thirty-five legal officers. When I retired in 2015 the figures were approximately 80,000 and 130 respectively; less danger of war but a lot more law.

So, in answer to the question which may be in the reader's mind, it was actually the law which brought me to Sandhurst that evening, as part of a small team of army legal officers visiting the academy to provide training in military law and LOAC to officer cadets.

Perhaps the next question is how and why on earth would somebody end up as a lawyer in uniform?

If you asked a soldier why he joined the army, or a lawyer why he chose the law as a career, their respective answers would probably be something like this:

The soldier: To get away from a boring or troublesome home life, to see the world, for the comradeship and adventure, peer pressure at a time of national crisis, an honoured family tradition, or some combination of the above.

The lawyer: It sounded interesting, it was guaranteed to make me a decent living, my mum or dad was a lawyer, or again a combination of such reasons.

Introduction

How many people end up pursuing careers for reasons which they can barely remember after a few years, through luck, or bad luck for that matter, or just a strong dose of naïveté (as in my case)?

As for many, it was my last year at school which called for some focus on the matter, but let's begin at the beginning.

My parents first met in 1936, emerging from the Second World War having been separated for almost its entirety. My father, a corporal in the Military Police was captured on the sand dunes of Calais, within sight of the white cliffs of Dover, on 25 May 1940, his 34th birthday, which was also the day when he should have reported for officer training at Aldershot, but for him '*ze var vass over*'. My mother had left her sheltered background working in the family 'Court Dressmaking' business for a commission in the Women's Auxiliary Air Force (WAAF), in which she spent a rather more glamorous war, culminating in a position on Air Chief Marshal Tedder's staff, and with an MBE for work in tracing V-1 'Doodlebug' launch sites.

They were married in 1946 within months of a joyful reunion and produced three boys, of which I am the youngest. Like most veterans my parents were justly proud of their war service but mostly just hugely relieved it was all over. Neither of them talked much about their experiences but when it came to my schooling, their choice of Wellington College was probably influenced by the school's military heritage.

Wellington College was founded in 1859 as a memorial to the 'Iron Duke', considered to be more useful than such alternative suggestions made at the time as a statue of him in every substantial town in the country (which people would probably be trying to pull down today), to provide a 'muscular Christian' education for the orphaned sons of army officers. Over the years the school had evolved into a typical public school at which all comers were welcome, subject to the Common Entrance exam, irrespective of any military connection, although favourable terms still applied to the sons (still no girls back then) of servicemen of any rank. Unsurprisingly, therefore, many of my contemporaries were from army backgrounds.

A number of the teaching staff had distinguished wartime records. The headmaster, Frank Fisher, whose father officiated as Archbishop of Canterbury at the Queen's coronation, held the MC as did another master, Peter Willey, who walked with a distinctive limp despite having one shoe built up, after sustaining a serious leg wound in action. My sixth-form history master, 'Jumbo' Curtis, an intellectual authority on chess and Shakespeare, had been a POW on the Burma railway. He had clearly suffered greatly, being permanently stooped and speaking with a rather high-pitched voice. Schoolboy mythology had it that he had 'lost one ball' during interrogation. This was never verified of course (least of all, why just one?).

The Wellington Combined Cadet Force (CCF), in which my housemaster, Richard Wood, was a leading light as a major, was extremely active. It represented all three armed services and featured among other fearsome weaponry an elastic-band-powered glider in the RAF section, gaining altitudes up to a dizzying six metres, as well as a full military band and even an annual naval field gun race commemorating the relief of Ladysmith during the Second Anglo-Boer War. My own CCF career was unremarkable, but I did enjoy my Wednesday afternoons in uniform.

So, on reaching that final 'A' level summer and wondering what to do next, the army had become an obvious item on the possible agenda. I was not convinced the army was for me in the long term, but what to do with 'A' levels in English, History and French? I had no interest in teaching, I was no historian and really hadn't a clue what to do, but a degree seemed like a good idea. The law sounded interesting and my (lucky) decent grades pointed that way, so the decision was made and I accepted a place to read law at Southampton University the following year. In the meantime, I was determined to do some travelling and try to earn a little money.

I learnt from Mr Wood that in those days the army could even provide a gap year. It was called a 'Short Service Limited Commission', the aim of which was to encourage potential graduates to experience an early sample of army life, with a view to signing up to a university cadetship. Applicants had to pass the Regular Commissions Board (RCB) at Westbury, Wilts, where it still resides, supposedly with a high pass mark to match high demand, and there were various medicals, and an interview for the preferred regiment.

If you cleared all those hurdles you were on course for RMAS, followed by a commitment of six to nine months' service. I had no particular regimental connections and to be honest I really just wanted to guarantee the most exotic travel experience. I applied to the Brigade of Gurkhas, which in those days had a large training establishment and several battalions based in Hong Kong.

Chapter 1

On Her Majesty's Legal Service

Having been accepted by the Second Battalion, the Seventh (Duke of Edinburgh's Own) Gurkha Rifles and, somewhat to my surprise, passed the RCB, I embarked on my three-week Sandhurst crash course, emerging still looking cringingly young for my age; I believe I do have a photograph to prove it somewhere but I shrink from publishing it. With a pip on each shoulder, I was officially a 'three week wonder', as we were slightly sardonically dubbed by our RMAS colour sergeant, and shortly after that I found myself on an RAF VC10 from Brize Norton bound for Hong Kong via RAF Gan.[1]

In those days the excitement of Hong Kong began with the landing at Kai Tak airport, flying down between apartment blocks, with washing suspended on bamboo poles seemingly inches from the wingtips, the pilot slamming on the brakes on touchdown to steer clear of the waters of the harbour awaiting you hungrily at the end of the short runway. Having survived that, I was met by a couple of subalterns from the battalion, who took me to tea at the Peninsula Hotel.[2]

In those days the Peninsula, in its prime location on Kowloon's waterfront (sadly today pushed inland by land reclamation), and with its fleet of bottle-green Rolls-Royce hotel taxis parked out front, was the place to be seen in Kowloon. The grand entrance led into an enormous, pillared lobby where guests enjoyed everything from English cream teas to literally whatever cocktail you could think of. A favourite sport would be to summon a waiter and order a ridiculously named cocktail, comprising an equally ridiculous blend of ingredients. Having been summoned to 'Bring me a Rancid Weasel, please', the waiter would assiduously note the ingredients of the unspeakable concoction as instructed, to be added to the repertoire at the bar for the future. Waiters scurried hither and thither carrying trays of orders with customers' names chalked on little blackboards on poles, ringing a bicycle bell to attract their attention.

We then headed up through Lion Rock Tunnel to the New Territories. Up here the country was a complete rural contrast to the rabbit warren of Kowloon, which even back then was a mega city of skyscrapers teeming with life and traffic. Queen's Hill Camp, Fanling, the home of 2/7 GR was a rambling establishment, largely comprising Nissen-hut-style buildings interspersed with parade grounds, sports pitches and vehicle parks, in the lee of steep, scrubby hillsides and surrounded by rather smelly duck farms.

My fellow officers, the youngest of whom was a good four years older than me, were very welcoming to this callow boy who had suddenly been foisted upon them. This was just as well, as my three-week wonder course had featured a fair bit of marching about and polishing things but otherwise added very little to what the CCF had already taught me about military life, which wasn't a lot either, to be honest. I had enjoyed the course but it had really done next to nothing to prepare me for the real thing.

The British first encountered the Gurkhas as a ferocious enemy on the northern frontier of the British Raj in the nineteenth century. It was because of their unique aptitude as infantrymen that we wisely decided that we needed them fighting for us, not against, and so the recruitment of these Nepali hill men into the Indian Army began in 1815.

Little seemed to have changed in the Gurkhas – sometimes rather rudely referred to by other regiments as 'White Officers with brown Privates'– from those days of the Raj. Thus, even my status at the very bottom of the British officer pile entitled me to the services of a full-time orderly. Sandhurst could have skipped all the polishing and pressing training because the superb and cheerful Lance-Corporal Rambahadur Gurung did it all for me, as he did my cleaning, washing and early morning cup of tea brewing.

Three mornings a week, at an hour which was already ridiculously hot and humid, another pre-breakfast event of an entirely different nature took place, a lung-searing four-mile run up hill and down dale between the duck farms and the Chinese squatter compounds, with their furious dogs hurling abuse at us. I had thought I was reasonably fit but I was small and skinny and the Gurkhas' famous stamina was in a different league. Most of the British officers had forced themselves, if not to lead, at least to keep up with these superhuman little hill men but for me it was an unequal struggle from which it seemed to take the rest of the day to recover.

The officers' mess, although unpromisingly housed in yet another glorified Nissen hut, was a delight inside, filled with military portraits and regimental silver, where all officers in station during the week were expected to assemble at 12.30 pm sharp for pre-lunch drinks. There was no bar, considered to be an institution only suitable for the sergeants' mess; but these were not the po-faced days of soft drinks and sandwiches, refreshment in Hong Kong's humid climate demanding at least a brace of ice-cold San Miguel lagers in chilled silver goblets,[3] produced in exchange for a chit by a white-liveried Gurkha mess waiter, followed by a three-course meal which was often a fantastic curry with all the trimmings.

On one occasion, which should be memorable but is actually strangely blurred, I was also formally introduced to the Queen's Gurkha Officers (QGOs). These very experienced officers, all long-serving soldiers commissioned from the ranks and led by the 'Gurkha Major', were the backbone of any Gurkha battalion, the *crème de la crème*, although technically junior to any British officer. I had been instructed that as a matter of courtesy I should pay my respects to the Gurkha Major and his QGOs by arranging to visit their mess, perched on a small hill in the middle of camp.

I duly arrived one evening and was treated like royalty, dining inevitably on 'Baht', Gurkha curry, which is pretty much all they eat. It is not particularly fiery but can still be a challenge as it always comes in huge portions, the meat being simply chopped, bone, gristle and all, accompanied by a rather slimy anonymous vegetable and a mountain of rice.

The resemblance to royalty ended abruptly when I was poured out of the building late in the evening, barely able to stagger down the hill, having been introduced unsuspectingly to large measures of Gurkha rum. I then circumnavigated camp several times in the dark in both directions before eventually stumbling upon my room and collapsing in bed fully dressed, until Rambahadur's insistent prodding, 'Sahib, Sahib!'[4] brought me round to a record-breaking headache the next morning; thank God it wasn't a running day.

The best times for me in Hong Kong were actually not spent in camp, but detached on other duties. I spent some weeks on the Chinese border, which was still very much the front line between the colony and Mau's Red Army. We had the benefit of occupying the high ground along the border, with a string of observation posts,[5] each manned by a rotation of sections of five or six soldiers under command of a sergeant, whose mission was meticulously to log anything that moved on the other side.

We were deposited at the foot of the hill, which was a blessing, as Gurkha drivers are terrifying enough even on the flat, and trekked up hundreds of steps to our little concrete bunker, with our kit brought up behind us by mule. There we spent happy days in the sun, left entirely in peace by the rest of the world, looking down into China through powerful binoculars. For hours on end every day we could hear loudspeakers broadcasting communist party propaganda across the paddy fields and we would watch groups of PLA soldiers huddled cross-legged in whatever shade they could find, with Mao's *Little Red Book* in their hands, being harangued by their officers.

Occasionally in the evening we would hear shots, as the PLA would kill anybody seen attempting to rush the flimsy barbed-wire border fence in a bid to escape to the freedom of Hong Kong and the West. Sometimes they would make it, to join the hordes of refugees in Hong Kong's squatter camps, where they were allowed to remain rather than face certain execution had they been sent back.

After border ops I moved from the sublime to the ridiculous, the fleshpots of downtown Hong Kong. This happened because HM Governor, Sir Murray MacLehose,[6] was at all times protected by a guard of honour at his residence, Flagstaff House, on Hong Kong Island. Although the guard, which rotated monthly, was often drawn from a Gurkha battalion, regulations required it to be commanded by a British officer, not a Gurkha. B Company 2/7 GR's turn came up to provide the guard and my OC, Major Colin Lees, decided that instead of taking himself off to Hong Kong, he might as well take advantage of having a buckshee Brit on his company strength so I was to be dispatched as guard commander while he remained in Fanling, using his time more gainfully back there. I had precisely zero knowledge of sword drill or other ceremonial etiquette but the actual work would all be done by the QGO, Captain Kulbahadur Mall, so what could possibly go wrong?

This suited me fine, as I was installed in a very comfortable room in the HQ officers' mess in Victoria Barracks, with minimal workload and maximum opportunity to explore Hong Kong and Kowloon, racing at Happy Valley courtesy of a Jardine's box-holder who was a friend of my mother's, and even the Macau casino, via hydrofoil. Thus followed a very enjoyable month, spending evenings with fellow officers from the HQ, crisscrossing the harbour on the Star Ferry, enjoying the music and discos of the day[7] in haunts such as the Go Down under the Furama Hotel, the Bull and Bear and the Yellow Submarine or visiting Sam's tailor in Nathan Road for fine next-day bespoke shirts, occasionally running the gauntlet of fleshpots like the Wanchai district.

One lunchtime in the mess bar one of my fellow officers, knowing I was an aspiring law student, introduced me to a Major John Taylor of the Army Legal Service Staff List.[8] We had a brief chat, but thinking nothing of it, I didn't see him again in Hong Kong, little knowing that our paths would cross just a few years later.

I was really only troubled by the guard on one occasion during the entire tour of duty. It must have been about 7 am, and I was still in bed when the phone rang. The fact that it happened at all was slightly surprising as I had been there for three weeks and it had never rung before; although I had been informed it was the duty phone, I had been rather hoping it was purely ornamental. It was effectively a 'hot line' from the guard so I picked it up a little gingerly, praying not to face some taxing 'command' decision.

Sure enough, it was Kulbahadur. We exchanged greetings; 'Good morning, Sahib, what can I do for you?'

'We want to know how to fly the Union flag this morning.'

'What do you mean?'

'President Pompidou has died, so we thought perhaps it should be at half-mast.'

Now this sounded like a bit of a tricky one, with all the hallmarks of a diplomatic disaster. I hadn't a clue what the etiquette was but I thought I knew a man who would, the governor's ADC.[9] 'OK, Captain K, it's a good question – let me check and I'll ring you back.'

I hung up and rang the ADC's number, which rang and rang for so long that I was about to hang up again when it was finally answered, by a slightly grumpy-sounding voice: 'Yes?'

''Er, good morning, it's Second Lieutenant Nelson speaking, is that the ADC?'

'No.'

'Ah … may I ask who is speaking, please?'

'It's the governor. Who are you?'

At this point I instantly shot up to attention at my bedside table and broke into a cold sweat, my voice now an octave higher: 'Oh, good morning Your Excellency, I'm so sorry to trouble you. I'm your guard commander and I was wondering if I could speak to your ADC.'

'I see. Well, I've no idea where he is, probably still in bed. Can I help?'

I then explained the query concerning the unfortunate demise of M. Pompidou, of which it transpired the governor had been as ignorant as me.

After a short pause, he replied, 'Oh, I see, yes that is a good question.' After a very brief moment of silent deliberation with himself, the governor advised, 'Oh, I think full mast as usual will be fine.'[10]

'Thank you, sir,' I squeaked.

I got back to Kulbahadur with his orders, before showering and getting dressed in record time in case any further nasty demands cropped up.

Shortly after my spell in the bright lights, I set off with B Company for four weeks of jungle warfare training in Brunei, on the island of Borneo, where there was, and still is to this day, a resident battalion of Gurkhas. This mutually convenient arrangement is paid for by the Sultan under a treaty which bolsters the Bruneian armed forces in maintaining the security of the small independent oil-rich state and provides the Gurkhas unlimited jungle warfare training and sunshine.

The capital, in the north of Brunei is Bandar Seri Begawan, or BSB. The Gurkha garrison is in Seria, a Royal Dutch Shell oil town in the south, and about halfway between the two lies the small town of Tutong, home to the jungle warfare training school. In those days, when so many British troops, principally Gurkhas, were based in Hong Kong, Tutong Camp was kept busy for several months every year with company-strength training cadres rotating in and out for a series of exercises.

That month was without question the most physically demanding experience of my life, teaching me three very clear lessons. First, that the Gurkhas are some of the finest soldiers on the planet, if not the finest; secondly, you do not want to go to war in the jungle; and thirdly, my career would not be in the 'poor bloody infantry'.

Tropical jungle is 'the most biodiverse terrestrial ecosystem on the planet'[11] and an absolutely fascinating environment. However, take it from me, it is bloody difficult to operate in at the best of times, with its combination of heat, humidity, rough terrain, bugs, bogs, leeches, thorns, the occasional snake, and the strange noises and total blackness of nights totally devoid of moon or starlight. Navigation is a nightmare, with visibility severely restricted even in daylight by secondary growth and a landscape dominated by forest giants, allowing no opportunity to identify landmarks to steer by.

We were struggling through it all for days on end with thirty kilos on our backs, maintaining 'tactical' silence, sometimes actually trying to charge an imaginary enemy in mock assaults and sometimes lying up hour after hour in a pool of sweat, waiting in ambush for him. We buried all traces of our presence and made no attempt at personal hygiene. This was not just unmilitary sloppiness by the way, but essential to maintain concealment, as unnatural smells like soap instantly give you away to the enemy at some distance in that environment.[12]

The Gurkhas' jungle fighting qualities came to the fore alongside the Chindits in Burma during the Second World War, and come 'Partition' in 1947 the newly independent Indian Army was determined to maintain a substantial number of them within its own ranks, many more in fact than we needed in the British Army.[13] By that time, however, a tradition of pride and prestige associated with serving in the British Indian Army had already developed, which, combined with lesser demand and a more rigorous selection process, has meant that the very best Gurkha soldiers tend to end up creamed off into the British Army.[14]

So, back to Brunei, and there was I, blundering about with my sub-machine gun and kukri, webbing chafing at my skinny, sweaty shoulders under the weight of my large pack, every muscle crying out for relief, and teeth gritted just trying to keep up and not make a complete arse of myself, never mind trying to be a 'leader of men'.

Meanwhile, the soldiers, also short in stature, and no more in their natural environment than me, literally took to the task like ducks to water, swarming effortlessly and silently through the secondary vegetation like a pack of Springer spaniels, grinning like school kids on a day out and making light work of troublesome creepers and lianas with their kukris.

Having set out on the day's gruelling route march at first light, we would stop at about midday and go 'non-tactical', i.e. you could make some noise and smoke. The Gurkhas' dietary requirements were blissfully simple. They just needed a mound of baht and rice twice a day, so at the lunch break they would immediately set about cooking up the first instalment of the day, which was provided in the form of a British army ration pack.

The faithful Rambahadur was even by my side in Brunei and I had been advised that either I could carry baht on exercise, in which case he would cook for me, or I could carry British rations,[15] in which case I was on my own. I liked baht, but not twice a day every day, and by lunchtime all I wanted to do was crash out under a tree with a cup of tea and an army biscuit, try and burn the leeches off my ankles with a cigarette end, and rest my aching body. I would also have felt a bit guilty expecting poor old Ram to cater for me as well as himself in the circumstances, so I opted for British rations.

The day's ordeal would usually finish at about 5 pm which would give us about two hours of daylight to 'harbour up', i.e. make camp and eat and clear up before turning in. It was always a bit of a race because the rapid tropical sunset was exaggerated by the dense primary jungle, so that you went from reasonable visibility to literally being unable to see your hand in front of your face within about ten minutes and, like any other luxury, torches were, naturally, forbidden.

Our activities at this time of day were accompanied by the amazingly loud voices of what sounded like donkeys flying through the forest canopy high above us. At first, we thought they were birds, which our Brit medical corporal drily identified in his heavy northern accent as 'drive you up the bloody wall birds'. In fact, they were no more birds than donkeys, but some sort of insect; I never did find out exactly what, but I agreed with the medic's verdict on the sound effect. As a contrast, in the morning we would sometimes be serenaded by hornbills or troupes of whooping gibbons, which were actually quite tuneful.

Our accommodation comprised individual *bashas*[16] made from saplings slung between more substantial tree trunks and covered with large leaves, sheltered against the occasional overnight rain by an overhead waterproof. Dear old Rambahadur insisted on making my *basha* every evening, which he invariably achieved in no time, and the combination of my exhaustion and his skill had me sleeping like the dead every night.

One evening, however, we were rather late harbouring up, and with the light fading fast I was concerned Ram would run out of time to sort himself out so I advised him, under strong protest, that I would make my own *basha* so that he could get on with his. I had watched him every evening so I was entirely confident that I knew exactly what to do and although my skill with the kukri was clearly limited (involving much bad language and frenzied hacking, unlike his unerring silent, surgical strokes), the finished product looked pretty good.

I soon found that looks can be very deceptive, as notwithstanding my usual state of weariness, I barely got a wink of sleep, with lumps and bumps emerging everywhere below, and a persistent leak from above. Matters went from bad to worse, as at some point in the pitch-black silence I could hear some unidentified animal scuffling about, sniffing and scratching itself, uncomfortably close to my personal patch of jungle. Every time I tried to frighten it off there would be silence for a minute, only for it to return from another direction. It was torture, because I couldn't shine a light and no amount of rational thinking that it could only be small, harmless and fearful of Man would put my mind at rest. Eventually I just had to block my ears until sleep came at last, seemingly about half an hour before being shaken awake by a grinning Rambahadur, armed with a mug of tea.

Despite its rigours, I survived this arduous adventure without injury or illness and enjoyed short periods of R&R in camp, or down in Seria, where we Gurkha officers enjoyed honorary membership of the beautifully appointed Panaga country club, owned and run by Shell for its executives, complete with outdoor pool, tennis, golf and several bars.

Our time in Brunei coincided with the club's summer ball but I nearly didn't make the party, as I seriously blotted my copybook with Major Lees. I had obviously watched too much of *Sgt. Bilko* in my youth as I had assumed it was OK for any officer to just turn up at MT[17] and borrow a vehicle, so one day I did just that, taking a Land Rover for a trip out on a mail and laundry run, with one or two others along for the ride.

On return from my jaunt, I soon learnt the error of my ways, finding myself summoned by the OC for an interview without coffee, severely bollocked, and threatened with the humiliation of an immediate return to Hong Kong. My plea in mitigation saw the sentence commuted to a ban on attending the big party, but when the OC later learnt that I had been unable to sell on my (rather expensive) ticket he relented further and there was some sort of rather academic confinement to camp instead, so like Cinderella I went to the ball after all. He was obviously more of a softy than he seemed.

The ball was a lavish black-tie affair at which much of the building was remodelled as the London Underground for nostalgic British ex-pats and the band of the Argyll and Sutherland Highlanders were flown over from Singapore to play, a memorable night like something out of *The Raj Quartet*.[18]

We threw our own party at Tutong on our last night in Brunei and I thought I should try to redeem my mediocre jungle performance with some contribution to the evening's programme, and ended up giving a rendition of 'Lili Marlene'. It took a moment for the penny to drop when I came on stage but when the Gurkhas, with their wonderful unsophisticated sense of humour, realized who the caterwauling idiot in drag was, they were beside themselves with hysterical laughter and applause at this sight of one of their Sahibs deliberately making such a fool of himself for their entertainment. As I bowed out, even the rather serious OC patted me on the back with a wink and a 'Well done, you've earnt your pay today'.

The following day we all jumped on buses for BSB, and the RAF flew us back to Hong Kong, where fond farewells took place over the next couple of weeks as my initial foray into military life came to an end and it was time to come back down to earth. The flight home went via a refuelling stop at RAF Akrotiri in Cyprus, which was in armed turmoil as Turkey had just invaded the north, so our stopover was conducted in record time.

I had loved my time with the Gurkhas, who were such wonderful people – tough, practical and above all hugely cheerful and fun to be around. However, I had decided not to pursue a university cadetship. I wasn't yet sure whether I would follow up my degree and become a lawyer but if I did, I would need to be free to work in Articles[19] or a Pupillage[20] after graduating, which would clash with commitment to the army were I a cadet. In any event I think the army and I had both concluded that although my Gurkha time had passed happily enough, I was no infantryman.

After the intensity of Hong Kong and Brunei, which had both been every bit as exciting and challenging as I could have hoped, life back with my parents in Kent was pretty dull and time rather dragged during the few weeks before the next move, the law degree. So, with that rite of passage behind me, I arrived at Southampton in late September, very excited to be away from home again and eager to discover what the law had to offer.

Talking to people over the years about their legal careers I never know whether to be comforted or surprised by how many of them clearly shared my ignorance of what legal practice entailed when they first set out to become lawyers. What few of us realized, and most laymen never get to discover, is how much of the law is incredibly tedious and dull and how little of it includes anything which might remotely be called exciting or glamorous. What's more, that most inflexible of all laws, 'Sod's Law', also ensures that the duller the legal specialization the more remunerative it is and conversely of course, the glamorous, exciting stuff is not well paid at all.

I had expected to spend my university years alternating between drinking lots of beer[21] and being mesmerized by lectures on the dramatic twists and turns in the evidence before the Old Bailey in cases such as Dr Crippen, the 'Brides in the Bath' and the Moors Murderers, so my first glimpse of the year one curriculum was rather a blow. In that first year there were no options; every subject was compulsory, including such delights as constitutional law, the law of trusts, property law, contract law, family law, revenue law, probate and succession, and something called legal method.[22] I turned and re-turned the pages several times looking for the criminal law syllabus before finally accepting that at least in year one, there was none.

By some twist of the marking system year two was the toughest, in which I think three subjects were compulsory, with another three to be chosen from a number of options. Here at last there was a bit of crime, the law of evidence. But some options were a lot tougher than others, and for those of us whose sole aim in life by then was to graduate by hook or by crook, tactics demanded the easier options. 'Evidence' was notoriously a tricky one and therefore to be avoided, whereas public international[23] law was not so bad. I hadn't really heard of that before but opted for it anyway along with other subjects which escape me now, and somehow, I was still afloat by the end of that crucial year two, still having yet to get the merest glimpse of Dr Crippen et al.

I remember year three for one subject in particular. It was another option, 'The carriage of goods by sea', a Southampton speciality, given its nautical connections, which sounded unusual and particularly appealing because it featured an 'open book' exam. My thinking was that if you spent an afternoon the day before the exam finding your way around the book in question and could then take it into the exam and just look up the answers, it had to be a dead cert for a First while also saving so much more of your life for important things like partying.

This proved to be seriously misguided, and the exam was a waking version one of those classic insecurity nightmares from which you awaken in a cold sweat, gasping and wondering why the sheets are twisted round your legs and the dog is trembling in the corner of the bedroom.

I must have spent two of the three hours of the exam frantically rifling through not just one but the two or three set 'open' books in desperation for some intelligent and substantial material to add to my candidate number at the top of the page. At the end of the exam, I emerged from a pile of crumpled A4 and ragged textbooks cursing my indolence and stupidity for thinking my cunning plan could ever have worked. However, either my paper became confused with some other unfortunate candidate's or I must have got something right without realizing it because I scraped a pass.

In year three we also all had to submit a 20,000-word dissertation on a legal topic of our choice. By the middle of the first term, we were getting near make-up-your-mind time for a subject and I was struggling for inspiration. Many of my contemporaries had some parental assistance; I remember one chap whose father was a Water Board executive, enabling easy access to research material on public sanitation law. I doubt his work was the greatest read but it passed muster. Another, who went on to a very successful banking career, wrote a prescient piece on insider trading, which few people seemed to have heard of in those days and which, amazingly, was still largely legal.

Finally, I got it. I had spent a month during the summer camping in Kenya with an old school friend and literally on my first night, at a campsite near Nairobi we had been very dramatically mugged at 'panga point', and were in fact very lucky to get away uninjured. By a further stroke of luck, unheard of in those parts, our three assailants were rapidly rounded up still in possession of all our belongings,[24] only to be severely beaten up by the police in our presence. Our holiday was then further interrupted a couple of weeks later when we attended Nairobi Crown Court to give evidence at the trial.[25] Several defendants were chained to a rail in the corner of the court, and as each case was called, they would be released and put in the dock, on a sort of production line. Meanwhile, in an interesting variation on a 'dock ID'[26] the senior police officer in our case, clearly keen to ensure that the unprecedented success of his case so far would continue to conviction, had us outside court with the door ajar, pointing at one of our three defendants and hissing in my ear, 'When the judge ask you which one had the panga, it is that one.'

Halfway through the trial, the judge,[27] who coincidentally knew my travelling companion Henry's family, called us into his chambers:

'I shouldn't really talk to you while the case is ongoing, but I just wanted to say what rotten luck it must have been for this to happen to you on your holiday, and do come to dinner when it's all over.'

In due course two out of the three defendants were convicted and sentenced to lengthy terms of imprisonment, combined in one case with corporal punishment. The third was acquitted, and a few days later Henry and I enjoyed a perfectly cooked impala steak with the judge.

I thought all this was much more interesting than the Water Board, so I submitted as my dissertation subject, 'The rule of law and human rights in Kenya post-independence', which I thoroughly enjoyed researching and writing. The judge happily contributed, and I also had a draft reviewed by the Principal of the Kenya Law School in Nairobi.[28] Unfortunately, my tutor, Dr Albie Sachs[29] who had the duty of marking it, was not entirely impressed with my rather critical conclusions but fortunately he was a scrupulously fair marker.

My three years at university flashed by so quickly that I still hadn't really made up my mind what came next, but having achieved a satisfactory grade,[30] I was eligible to study for the Law Society's part two solicitors' exams. Thus, after another gap year spent travelling, I found myself in the summer of 1978 reporting for duty at the College of Law, Braboeuf Manor, Guildford.

If there were times at university when I found studying law a painful experience, nothing there had prepared me for the six months of cramming administered at law school. The methodology can only have been devised as some sort of Neo-Darwinian process to weed out the insufficiently committed. This was a proper six months' full-time job, setting the uncivilized tone by starting in August, when the rest of the world, especially the student world, was enjoying high summer, with not so much as a long weekend off until the short Christmas break and then exams in February. During that period the material to be digested must have been at least double the three years' worth at university. Students were assigned to either morning or afternoon lectures, on six legal subjects, each lecture lasting an hour. In fact, they were really not lectures at all, but dictation sessions, with the 'lecturer' beginning each session with something like: 'Commercial Law, Heading – Large Roman I, Subheading – Capital A. – Consumer Credit, next line, Little 1.) –Debtor/ Creditor/ Supplier Agreements ...'

And so, the hour proceeded, with thirty or so *automata* frantically scribbling verbatim every word uttered by the dictator (at least I learnt what that word meant). There was no discourse or explanation; the name of the game was to equip yourself with four hours' worth of notes by the end of the morning or afternoon (whichever straw you had drawn), and then return, already exhausted, to your digs and try and make some sense of it all, 'assisted' by the relevant textbooks in time to start again the next day.

Woe betide you if your pen packed up or you had to stop to scratch your nose, let alone attend to nature's call during a lecture; the dictation juggernaut stopped for nobody and once you'd missed a passage there was no going back. Indeed, the pace was such that even your fellow victims were usually unable to help you fill gaps in the aftermath; you just had to try and guess what you'd missed.

Everyone was so ground down by this regime that there was literally no light relief, and unlike university most people just spent their weekends catching up on their sleep rather than socializing. I started to form a very unfair impression of the people with whom I had elected to share a career, as they all seemed a pretty dull bunch but I later realized that the poor sods were in fact, like me, just too anxious and exhausted to enjoy themselves. OK, it wasn't the Gulag archipelago, but it certainly wasn't any fun.

Although I am not a 'morning person' I was saved by the fact that I had morning lectures, because if I had been subjected to this daily marathon in the afternoon, I would have run out of steam for any analysis later in the day, quite apart from even trying to interpret my own handwriting, which was bad at the best of times but now destruction-tested. By the next morning any vague grasp of the previous day's double Dutch would have been lost forever. As it happened, I was able to stagger home and, after drawing breath at lunchtime, steel myself to the afternoon's brain ache with at least some remnant of mental energy available.

When February came round, I took the advice of a friend who had crashed and burned the previous year, and exercised my right to defer one of the six exams[31] in order to improve my chances on the others. I had already decided that for me the Neo-Darwinism had worked and had I fallen at that hurdle I was not going back to square one, and would turn to something other than the law, but although I was left with a couple of re-sits and the dreaded solicitors' accounts exam to knock off, I squeezed through enough to keep going.

I could now look for somebody foolish enough to take me on as an articled clerk and I soon found myself invited for an interview with

Arthur Dixon, the senior partner of a small Southampton firm, and was taken on. The contact came through a friend at the Bar, the interview took place over a cup of tea at Arthur's home, and the offer of the job came over the phone the next morning, at the princely salary of £1500 per annum.[32] How times have changed; there was no Linkedin, no fifteen-page application form, no personal statement, no Disclosure and Barring police certification to prove I was not a paedophile, not even a requirement to disclose my ethnicity or sexual orientation, and in fact I don't think I was even asked for a CV or evidence of my degree or Part 2 exams.

I must say it wasn't the most illustrious firm, or the highest-quality articles. My desk was in the corner of Arthur's office, adding to the Dickensian atmosphere of the Victorian terrace which the firm occupied, and my ability to concentrate on my work was seriously jeopardized by his manic pacing up and down the room, jabbering loudly into a Dictaphone. Fortunately, this was often relieved by his frequent long boozy lunches out with some decidedly dubious clients, early departures in the afternoon, and the occasional flip from Eastleigh airport to Jersey for a day out on some (allegedly) nefarious business which was never discussed in the office.

After an impoverished and depressing year of this, during which my initial doubts about the law as a career were reinforced daily on a monotonous diet largely consisting of conveyancing followed by more conveyancing, I was offered a magnificent pay rise to £1,850 per annum[33]. But I had dug my escape tunnel; my university friend Greg, who had previously been in articles with a neighbouring firm, had recently moved to London and called me out of the blue one day, suggesting I apply for a vacancy with his new employers, who, he assured me, would offer £4,000 to the successful candidate, which, after another short interview, was me.

I left that London office one Friday at the end of my two years' articles and walked back in on the Monday as a solicitor, now earning £7,000 per annum and basking in a warm glow of relief – I had made it, and like a delighted newlywed wife repeatedly reminding herself of her new surname, I found myself smiling inanely from time to time over the next few days as I reminded myself almost out loud, 'You're a solicitor!'

But apart from the pay, nothing else really changed much and after a while I began to think, OK, so what next? I was only 25 and I soon began to get itchy feet. The prospect of spending the next forty years commuting to and fro through the Blackwall Tunnel to the same office and to the life led by the middle-aged partners in the firm left me rather panic-stricken. Thinking back to my more exciting Hong Kong days, I remembered John Taylor,[34] and decided to find out a bit more about the Army Legal Corps.

To cut a long story short, less than twelve months after qualifying as a lawyer I was back at Sandhurst on the aptly nicknamed 'Vicars and Tarts' course. This was very similar in content to my previous incarnation there, but instead of spotty teenagers it was populated by officers to be commissioned into the professionally qualified corps – the medics, dentists, nurses, chaplains, lawyers and vets. It made for an interesting mix, including highly qualified, overweight consultants in their mid-40s, a chaplain[35] who was hugely disappointed that he was only allowed to carry a stick on exercises and not a machine gun, and my barrister friend Neil Jones. He was deliberately as camp as a row of tents, insisting that he would manage fine by reaching a 'reasonable compromise' with the 'staff' (who hadn't the first idea how to handle him and for whom the notion of any compromise was totally alien), on the subject of 'costume', and who seemed to be smuggling a roster of female acolytes into Victory College most evenings to polish his kit and resupply Mars Bars for the entire company.

Within a matter of weeks of my joining the ALC, the UK was at war with Argentina, but in those days none of the armed services saw any need for legal advisers in the field on such operations. Our main preoccupation was military discipline, and the lawyers' work was cut out advising COs on summary disciplinary matters and prosecuting at courts martial.

Having said that, my first full tour as a new captain was in Northern Ireland, itself a very active operational theatre at the time. One of my duties was as 'flying lawyer', spending alternate weeks on a 24/7 call-out roster to act as defence solicitor for soldiers under investigation by the RUC[36] following shooting incidents. This was quite a challenge, particularly since there was little opportunity at that time for the ALC to provide much in the way of 'induction training' for the transition from civilian to military legal practice. In good old British Army style you just had to pick things up as you went along.

However, I rapidly concluded that clattering across South Armagh in a Wessex[37] in the middle of the night to meet my client at some remote and heavily fortified police station in the aftermath of a terrorist contact was pretty good fun. It certainly beat the hell out of appearing before the grumpy County Court judge in Stratford E15, drafting affidavits for ouster injunctions against violent husbands, whose wives just let them back home the next week anyway, or filling in legal aid 'Green Forms'.

I loved the *frisson* of excitement driving the anonymous office Mini with its ever-changing number plates, and my cocked Browning pistol in the door pocket through the badlands of the Glenshane Pass[38] over to Derry to conduct a 'Legal Aid' clinic for soldiers in Ebrington Barracks, or sitting cramped in the back of a 'Pig'[39] en route to interview a client in West Belfast with bricks pinging off the armour plate. It made a great change from sitting in a traffic jam on the A2 on the way to work on a wet Tuesday morning; combine this with great camaraderie in the HQ mess, and as a way of life, there was no comparison.

During off-duty periods I would sometimes sit up in the HQNI ops room with the watch keepers, listening to contact reports from units on the ground and learning how the 'Teeth Arms' of the army function, in tense and sometimes bloody confrontation. I was in my element, my brief spell with the infantry providing a disproportionate boost to my confidence and comfort in the military environment, albeit doing a completely different job.

Many of my ALC colleagues had considerably more previous military experience than me. Major Jeremy Moon was my immediate superior in Northern Ireland, a Scottish solicitor and former cavalry officer straight out of Evelyn Waugh's *Sword of Honour* trilogy. He regularly rode to hounds somewhere different every weekend, amongst who knows what dubious characters and with a healthy disdain for the army's 'tribal' map. This was an official publication displayed on every office wall, warning of the danger areas of Northern Ireland to be avoided, by means of a colour-coding system from bright green to bright orange, indicating local republican or loyalist politico-religious affiliations.[40]

Whether or not they had the benefit of such previous military lives, most of my ALC contemporaries, whether barristers or solicitors, felt to me like fellow souls. Each had an affection for the law as a worthwhile profession and the army as an institution, invariably adventurous, restless and outgoing, a far cry from those down-trodden souls, including me, back in Guildford just a few years before, wondering what on earth they had got themselves into.

Over the following years I worked my way through a number of appointments, until in early 1997 I found myself setting up shop in Rochdale Barracks, Bielefeld, Nord Rhine Westphalia. This was the office of the newly established Army Prosecuting Authority (Germany) (APA(G)), where I had been posted as a major, and full-time prosecutor. My family accompanied me, and we settled happily into a spacious army quarter in the suburb of Heepen, with my son Philip at school in Catterick Barracks just up the road. By this time, I had already been a prosecutor for some years but still enjoyed the work and looked forward to a good two-year tour, hopefully with promotion in post.

A few months later I got a phone call from my friend Phil McEvoy whom I had met on day one at Sandhurst and who was now a lieutenant-colonel working for DALS.[41]

'Hi Jim, have you thought about your next posting?'

'I wasn't expecting to go anywhere for a while.'

'Well, you're due promotion in January and you can't stay there because there's no vacancy there for a half colonel'

'Oh, OK, so what are you offering?'

'We're thinking about the ICTY.'[42]

'Sounds all right, just let me know the details nearer the time.'

Although a bit of a bolt from the blue, this sounded quite an exciting idea – a couple of years in the Netherlands, and the job would fit my prosecuting background well, while getting me away from domestic crime and into some interesting international legal business.

However, it was not to be, as the incumbent in the post, Major Andrew Cayley[43] resigned his commission in ALS and secured the slot on the ICTY establishment as a civilian.[44] Phil rang me to tell me this news.

'Not to worry, these things happen, is there a Plan B?'

'How about the ARRC?'[45]

'OK, but isn't that all international and operational stuff?'

'Yeah, but you can cuff it'.

'I'll give it a go.'

And so, one day in the autumn of that same year I drove over to Rheindahlen, a large British base near Monchengladbach, between Dusseldorf and the Dutch border, which was home to HQ British Forces (Germany) and HQ Allied Rapid Reaction Corps (ARRC), to be shown around by Lieutenant-Colonel David Reddin, from whom I was posted to take over as Legal Adviser HQ ARRC on promotion in January 1998.

Chapter 2

Audentis Fortuna Iuvat

NATO was born in 1949 with the ratification of the Washington Treaty by all original twelve member states. Its raison d'être was, in a nutshell, to deter aggression against the West and in particular the mutual, 'collective' defence by any or all of its member states of one another in the event of an armed attack. This is spelt out in Article 5 of the treaty, as follows:

> The Parties agree that an armed attack against one or more of them in Europe or North America shall be considered an attack against them all and consequently they agree that, if such an armed attack occurs, each of them, in exercise of the right of individual or collective self-defence recognized by Article 51 of the Charter of the United Nations, will assist the Party or Parties so attacked by taking forthwith, individually and in concert with the other Parties, such action as it deems necessary, including the use of armed force, to restore and maintain the security of the North Atlantic area.[1]

The genesis of this arrangement so soon after the Second World War was no coincidence, with the urgent need to safeguard the West from the expansionism of the Warsaw Pact which was clear for all to see. From that time until the collapse of the 'Iron Curtain' in the early 1990s, tens of thousands of NATO troops, particularly British and American, were permanently on duty in West Germany and beyond, on that mission. However, with that collapse everything changed, some even arguing that NATO, having triumphed without a shot being fired, had become redundant.

However, over those forty years NATO had grown into a substantial political as well as military juggernaut, in fact the largest military alliance in history, and despite the apparent demise of the threat from the East there was never any realistic prospect of its dissolution. Indeed, much to the discomfort of Moscow, NATO continued to expand rapidly eastward as one by one many of the countries recently relieved of the Soviet yoke sought shelter against its return under the umbrella of NATO membership.[2] It was apparent that the organization needed to adapt to the changed world around it. This called for a restructuring, from entrenchment on the North German Plain, with its weapons, like the guns of Singapore in 1942 all trained unflinchingly in one direction, to a more agile NATO, ready to adjust its arcs of fire and redeploy manpower and matériel in unpredictable directions.

Out of this restructuring the Allied Rapid Reaction Corps[3] emerged. For most of the time the ARRC exists as a 'virtual' corps, the only permanently established bit being the HQ, of about 400 personnel, with administrative support provided by the (British) ARRC Support Battalion, itself a bit of a misnomer, being nothing like a conventional-strength battalion. The fighting body of the corps comprises units of the armed land forces of a variety of NATO member states under national command, coming together from time to time to train, and if called upon, fight, under NATO ARRC command. As it says on the tin, the idea is that this structure is prepared, through a combination of regular training, liaison and prepositioned command plugs and sockets to coalesce into an effective land fighting force to react rapidly to any armed attack or threat against NATO or her allies.

The UK is the so-called 'framework nation' for the ARRC, meaning that the UK provides the lion's share of its funding and about 60 per cent of the HQ personnel including the Commander, a lieutenant-general and the Chief of Staff, a major-general. Various other key appointments are also 'flagged' by certain nations, such as the deputy commander's post, an Italian major-general[4], and the senior Operations (G3) post, a US brigadier-general.

The ARRC formed up in 1992, initially inheriting the premises which had been occupied by the now defunct 1st British Corps in Ripon Barracks, Bielefeld, then moving in 1994 to Rheindahlen, not least as a more 'internationally equitable' location for this multinational establishment, nearer the Dutch and Belgian borders. With NATO HQ in Brussels and its military HQ, SHAPE,[5] in Mons, also Belgium, the new location was to prove very much more convenient for short-notice meetings across various levels of command during operational planning.

Audentis Fortuna Iuvat

For the British staff and their families, the new location, a good two hours closer to the channel by road, was also a great advantage.

The Rheindahlen military complex was built between 1952 and 1954, designed by a water-divining Royal Engineers colonel and completed in record time to ensure its funding came from the post-war German budget rather than the British taxpayer. It originally housed the British Joint (Army and RAF) HQ on the Rhine. The main building, variously known as 'the Big House' or 'the Kremlin', at 300 metres long by 180 wide was then reputedly the largest office building in Europe. It was an impressive rabbit warren of offices, luxurious in fact for senior officers, but by the time the ARRC arrived forty years later to occupy the first floor, most of the office accommodation was getting rather tired and challenging for adaptation to modern office IT and other infrastructure.[6]

Despite, or maybe because of, its vintage the camp itself was every serviceman's favourite place to live and work. It was originally established in a forested area of about 1,000 acres and had largely been preserved as a green and pleasant estate. This was bisected by the wide and scenic Queen's Avenue, with an Olympic-standard open-air swimming pool on one side and the Globe cinema opposite. There was an enormous NAAFI, an American PX, tax-free car showrooms, primary and secondary service schools, excellent sports pitches, tennis courts and facilities including a gym and a saddle club, spacious messes and even an excellent fish and chip shop. The service quarters were spacious and well laid out, within easy walking distance to work or school. In fact, it was just like home, only better.

The ARRC, motto, *Audentis Fortuna Iuvat*, meaning 'fortune favours the bold',[7] prided itself on being at that time NATO's only high-readiness land force,[8] and had already been blooded in the field in Bosnia in 1996. As such, an appointment on its staff was much sought after throughout the NATO contributing nations' armed forces, seen as an exciting working environment, financially advantageous in many cases,[9] and a good career move.

One intended consequence of this was that most of the staff, of whatever nationality, tended to be very high-quality operators. I don't mean to include myself in that number; there are exceptions to every rule, and I was there largely out of luck. However that may be, I could immediately tell that this was a step up from the relatively sleepy hollow of the APA and even before the prospect of another operational deployment arose, there seemed to be a buzz in the air. Then, within days of my arrival at JHQ, the commander, universally known by the abbreviation COMARRC, the hugely experienced General (shortly to become Sir) Mike Jackson delivered a New Year address in the garrison theatre which concluded with the injunction, 'Watch Kosovo', to which the reaction of many in the audience was, 'Where the hell is Kosovo?'

For me, the move also meant at least three major changes in working life. First, I was a lieutenant-colonel overnight, something which took a few weeks to get used to, rather like that transition from articled clerk to solicitor many years before[10] and in a way equally significant. Most officers can reasonably expect to reach the rank of major if they serve for any length of time, but beyond that the odds lengthen, so lieutenant-colonel is an important promotion, bringing an expectation that you are a proper 'grown-up'. To add to this already slightly daunting situation, my first client in the job was General Jackson, or 'Jacko' as he was affectionately known. I was acutely aware that you don't get to be a three-star corps commander without being a very clever guy, and in his case, despite his natural charm, there was a reputation for 'taking no prisoners,'[11] hence his nicknames of 'Darth Vader' or 'The Prince of Darkness', both of which, assuming he knew, he would have loved.

Secondly, not only did I have to adapt rapidly to my new seniority, but I was way out of my professional comfort zone. Whilst I had always found the military legal discipline of 'operational law' interesting, I had spent the vast majority of my career dealing with national military law, especially court-martial work. Even my Northern Ireland experience many years earlier was scant preparation for an appointment as the senior legal officer in this multinational corps HQ environment. Such was the slightly parochial business of much of the ALS organization in those days that unlike the vast majority of my 'mainstream' military colleagues, I had no military staff college qualifications at any level to my name.

Finally, I found that I had also moved into a new technological era, from one where I had dictated all my advices and correspondence, to be typed up from a tape by a real live typist and returned to me by email to polish, print and sign. Here I was in the brave new world of IT, requiring the rapid acquisition of the modern way of working, including learning to type. I had been around just about long enough to get my head round the British Army's command structure 'wiring diagrams', and the ubiquitous acronyms for which it is renowned, but here again

I had to start afresh. Not only did NATO apparently have an insatiable appetite for restructuring itself, with which it was hard to keep up, and although its conventional lingua franca is English, there was a whole new language of acronyms and abbreviations out there to be learnt if I was to have any hope of finding out what the hell was going on, and then staying afloat.

So, after a few days 'handover/takeover' from David Reddin, who tried to make sure I met all the people I needed to know and bring me up to speed with the business of the legal office, I formally assumed the appointment of 'Chief Legal'.

I was extremely lucky to inherit a Dutch legal officer, Major Wiebe Baron, as SO2[12] Legal. Wiebe, who had served with the ARRC on the Bosnia operation, not only therefore had the benefit of invaluable experience but was a great example of the high quality of many of the staff in the HQ. Like all Dutchmen he spoke and wrote perfect English, but he also proved to be a clever lawyer, IT whizz kid, and hugely industrious and enthusiastic all-rounder, who in later life went on to be ADC to Queen Beatrix of the Netherlands. I truly don't know what I would have done without him in those early days.

It soon became apparent just how complex an organization the ARRC was; with twenty different NATO member nations contributing staff to the HQ, it took a long time for anybody, let alone a NATO new boy to recognize what uniform came from where, and more importantly what insignia denoted what rank. The working atmosphere, although very professional was not unduly formal but that did not entirely alleviate the risk of inadvertently giving offence, purely out of ignorance.

During my handover/takeover I was literally on the threshold of the US one star's[13] office to introduce myself, having mentally prepared offering my hand with a polite 'Good afternoon, brigadier' when an alarm went off in my head. The British Army has for a hundred years always titled one-star officers 'brigadier' although historically the rank was brigadier-general, abbreviated to 'general'. Something warned me the US still used the old title, and, panicking slightly, I turned to David, 'What do I call him?' David could have had a lot of fun with this, but being a good chap, he did the decent thing and replied 'You call him "general".'

The door opened behind me, 'Good afternoon. Jim, isn't it?'

'Yes, good afternoon, general.' Thank God I checked, that could have been a bit embarrassing.

'Well, Jim, of course I'm pleased for you that you have all your limbs intact but to be honest I really prefer a one-handed lawyer.'

This seemed a rather strange introduction. 'OK ... why's that, sir?'

'Because I've always found when I ask a lawyer his advice, he'll say, "Well, on the one hand you could do this but on the other ..."' He was a real gentleman and we got on extremely well from the start.

Finding my way around this maze was pretty time consuming for several weeks, so it was fortunate that the weekly workload for the legal office was normally quite manageable but it wasn't long before the first of the HQ's heavy annual timetable of major staff exercises came around. Among other things, such exercises are designed to inflict maximum embuggerance on the HQ staff to test their adaptability to the fog of war, which was achieved in a variety of ways.

First, starting weeks before the actual exercise there were the endless planning meetings, demanding maximum attendance, often largely to enhance the profile of each planner's input. I soon learnt the value of applying a fine filter to such attendance but then there was the deluge of digital information distributed by an email scatter gun to all and sundry, with a daily amended diet of plans, annexes, contingencies, establishment tables and more plans, most of which also required judicious application of the 'delete' button.

The legal stuff for exercises tended to be relatively limited, dealing with such issues as rules of engagement and various imaginary instruments such as UN Security Council resolutions, technical agreements, memoranda of understanding and ceasefire agreements. It was during such exercises that the thrusting 'Teeth Arm' ARRC officer could seize the opportunity to shine, for example during the frequent 'Commander's briefings'. However, it soon became clear to me that the legal input was of marginally less interest than the weather report for purposes of exercise play, especially if such 'legal dick-dancing', of which I was once rather cheekily accused,[14] threatened the march to imaginary victory.

Then there would be the deployment to the exercise location itself, typically to a long-disused barracks complex which, despite the sterling efforts of the support battalion and the signallers, would invariably be cold, dusty, uncomfortable and plagued by poor communications and internet outages. Alternatively, such exercises have been known to take place in tents in the carpark, which is almost worse because from there you can look longingly up at the windows of your real office.

Audentis Fortuna Iuvat

To make it even more fun the working day would either require twenty-four-hour manning, or start at an uncivilized hour and tend not to finish until people thought there was nobody senior about to notice them slinking off to their bunk, having long since finished doing any actual work but not wanting to be seen to quit. Then, inevitably the last of the seven days or so would be conducted in full NBC[15] kit, which is unbelievably hot, sweaty and generally unpleasant to work in.

Just to complicate things further, the HQ was divided into two different locations, 'Main' and 'Rear', making twenty-four-hour manning for branches like mine with a grand total of two officers split between the two HQs, interesting to put it mildly. Fortunately, the operational establishment allowed for some augmentation and I was usually joined in Main by Captain Mark Dakers, an ALS colleague who left his day job back at Bielefeld for the duration to help out. He usually took the night shift and not only kept me on the straight and narrow with unfamiliar IT but helped ensure that my contribution to the commander's morning 'prayers' made a degree of sense. 'Face time' with the commander was a double-edged sword and even if the level of interest in the legal update usually attracted little more than a polite nod, it was as well to be prepared for cross-examination,[16] upon which the schadenfreude was very evident on the faces of others present.

Little did we know how closely a lot of this, often infuriating, make believe would be replicated for real within a matter of months, but in the autumn of 1998 the ARRC's principal annual exercise, 'ARRCADE Fusion',[17] had an air of schizophrenia about it because its fictional scenario (which, funnily enough, was Southern Iraq) was being played out against a backdrop of real-time events in the Kosovo region.

Life at HQ ARRC was by no means all work and no play, with the planning and training routine liberally interspersed with a variety of social and sporting events which were invariably well organized and well attended. The summer of 1998 was almost like one of those rose-tinted childhood summers, with such events as the annual Rheindahlen Summer Show held under balmy, cloudless skies.

The ARRC officers' mess was run by the Brits, and regarded as something of a diplomatic showpiece for our NATO colleagues to enjoy, so not only were the food and service top notch but the entertainment fund was generous. Every Friday featured a 6 pm 'Happy Hour' to which officers were invited with their families, friends, and of course, being a

British mess, dogs, for the sort of informal curry evening which only the British Army can do properly.[18] Each nation was also expected to lay on a party to celebrate its national day and given that about twenty nations were represented, this made for a lot of parties, with each national host competing to show off food, drink, costume and culture.

The main annual event hosted by the mess was the summer ball. This featured, as the centrepiece in the anteroom, a large vibrating bed (only in Germany!). Guests of either sex were invited to fling themselves on it, simulating carnal ecstasy for the entertainment of others. The gusto and realism with which this opportunity was seized, particularly by senior officers' wives of all nationalities, in magnificent evening dresses, was an eye-opener.

The spirit of competition runs through everything the British army does, of course, and ARRC personnel of all nations were encouraged to join in well beyond the social sphere. The occupancy of the gym was fairly representative of the respective importance attributed to physical training by different nations, where you couldn't move without tripping over Americans, but did not see too many from 'Club Med', our affectionate nickname for NATO colleagues from that part of the world.

However, when the chief of staff decided an inter-branch triathlon was to be held, maximum participation was expected. I was happy enough with this, although simple maths suggested that somebody in the legal branch was going to have to do two-thirds of the event. I rather thought this probably ought to be my younger and presumably fitter Dutch colleague, by now no longer Wiebe Baron but another agreeable Dutchman called Bart. However, the Dutch military had firm views not only on such matters as hair length, trades unions and working hours but, it seemed, also on extra-curricular activities. So somewhat to my surprise I found the legal branch triathlon team was ... me.

Fortunately, this was not a full-length Olympic-standard event and despite being so exhausted that by the time I got to the swim, which came last and where I almost drowned, I did just make it all the way round. I was a little disappointed there was no prize for the sole competitor in the event to have done the whole thing.

That wonderful summer weather was not unblemished, however, as storm clouds were gathering over the Balkans once again. Yugoslavia had been falling apart for many years, with ethnic divisions which had been papered over under Tito's regime laid bare and often bloody following the disintegration of the Eastern bloc. Kosovo, a province of Serbia bordered by Albania to the west and Macedonia, or 'FYROM' as we had to call it,[19] to the south, was increasingly becoming a tinderbox of tension between its majority Muslim ethnic Albanian population and the Christian Slavic Serbs governing them.

For many Serbs, Kosovo was the precious historic cradle of their nation but for Albanians it was seen as a territory destined to be the obvious prize of a 'Greater Albania'. Kosovar Serbs, represented in uniform by the Yugoslav Ministry of Internal Affairs Police[20] and the Yugoslav Army[21] were encouraged in their suppression of such an unwelcome notion by Yugoslav President Slobodan Milosevic, who despite presiding over Serbia's disastrous Balkan wars, still enjoyed heroic status among them.

On the other hand, the Albanian camp was seen widely in the West as an unjustly oppressed minority, not least among their diaspora in the US, who were typically generous in their provision of funding, moral support and probably weapons. Assisted and encouraged by this widespread condonation of their cause, the Albanian Kosovar guerrillas, the KLA,[22] were conducting an increasingly bold armed insurrection, provoking brutal reprisals by the Serbs and an existential crisis amongst the civilian population caught in the crossfire.

The international political backdrop for this delicate situation only increased the likelihood of escalation. In October 1998, impeachment proceedings were commenced against President Bill Clinton following allegations of sexual impropriety with the intern Monica Lewinsky – remember 'I did not have sexual relations with that woman'? – and it may not be unduly cynical to conclude that his apparent concern over developments in a little-known corner of central Europe, eagerly supported by Secretary of State Madeleine Allbright[23] had as much to do with a wish to redirect the spotlight as genuine humanitarian angst.

In the UK the bright-eyed young PM Tony Blair, in office for little over a year, had apparently also spied an opportunity to burnish his credentials as international statesman and human rights champion. Meanwhile, Yeltsin's economically troubled Russia unequivocally lent tacit support to her Serb friends, following the precedent of 1914, adding an ominous East/West tension to events as they unfolded.

A number of initiatives during the summer and autumn of 1998 such as the establishment of a UN-sanctioned monitoring force in Kosovo helped to calm the situation but the KLA clearly had the bit between their teeth and the level of violence inexorably continued to rise. NATO's SACEUR,[24] General Wesley Clark, a Vietnam veteran and old Bosnia hand, was no admirer of Milosevic, with whom perhaps he felt he had unfinished business, and before long the sound of rattling sabres grew louder and louder in NATO's corridors of power.

It rapidly became apparent that any military intervention against the Serbs was likely to be led by the ARRC, where the reaction of staff was, predictably, mixed. For many, the prospect of mobilization in a significant and possibly hazardous ground offensive was manna from heaven, just the sort of operation for which they had joined the army and a fantastic opportunity for a once-in-a-lifetime adrenalin rush, fame, fortune, medals and promotion.

For the more cautious there were real concerns about the 'justness' of the cause: were the Serbs really unequivocally and incorrigibly such bad guys or was the world in danger of being conned by a bunch of opportunistic Albanian mobsters? And whatever the answer to that question, were we not risking the West allowing its military arm, NATO, to be caught in a mangle which would also draw in the old adversary, Russia, sparking the third major conflagration in Europe in a century?

By Christmas 1998 I had begun to receive quite a stream of visitors to my office seeking a legal view on the likelihood of any such operation being allowed to happen.

Nobody should be surprised to find that the law of armed conflict,[25] also known as 'international humanitarian law', is extremely complicated, but in one particular respect it is remarkably simple; it is divided into those provisions dealing with the legality of embarking on armed conflict in the first place (which used to be called 'going to war'), the *ius ad bellum*, and those dealing with conflict once it has broken out, the *ius in bello*. Once battle has been joined, the parties are bound by the *ius in bello* whether or not the outbreak of conflict was lawful, but the question I was being asked concerned that first hurdle.

The modern *ius ad bellum* is contained within the Charter of the United Nations[26] by which all nations are bound, whose fundamental purpose is 'To maintain international peace and security'.[27] Decisions on matters such as the use of force are taken on behalf of the UN by the Security Council.

Audentis Fortuna Iuvat

Within the UN Charter:

Chapter I. provides:

Art 2(4)
All Members shall refrain in their international relations from the threat or use of force against the territorial integrity or political independence of any state, or in any other manner inconsistent with the Purposes of the United Nations.

Chapter VII deals specifically with the matter of use of force in two particular articles:

Art 42
Should the Security Council consider that measures provided for in Article 41[28] would be inadequate or have proved to be inadequate, it may take such action by air, sea, or land forces as may be necessary to maintain or restore international peace and security. Such action may include demonstrations, blockade, and other preparations by air, sea, or land forces of members of the United Nations.

And secondly, codifying the ancient customary law of self-defence there is:

Art 51
Nothing in the present Charter shall impair the inherent right of individual or collective self-defence if an armed attack occurs against a Member of the United Nations, until the Security Council has taken measures necessary to maintain international peace and security.

So, my (naïve as it turned out) answer to the question 'Could this legally happen?' was very clear, but bear with me.

Membership of the Security Council is rotational for most members of the UN but there are five permanent members: USA, Russia, UK, France and China.[29] In order to be passed, a motion put before the Security Council must, among other things, be supported by all those five permanent members. On the matter of use of force against Serbia in order to relieve the situation in Kosovo it was crystal clear that neither Russia nor China would support any such motion. Lawful use of force in accordance with a UNSC resolution under Article 42 was therefore out of the question because no such motion could be passed.

Turning to self-defence in accordance with Article 51, it was equally clear that, however violent the internal conflict between the protagonists within Kosovo might be from time to time, there existed no threat of an armed attack by Yugoslavia against any other UN member state which might justify the use of force against her in self-defence.[30]

Therefore, *QED*, NATO being a law-abiding organization, it would not be engaging in armed operations against Serbia on the basis of the situation in Kosovo because there could be no legal justification for any such action in accordance with international law.

Having said that, whatever I and my fellow uniformed lawyers might think had no bearing on the high politics at play, but winter in the Balkans is no 'fighting season' and so things went quiet in Kosovo for a few months. Meanwhile, however, the NATO planning super-tanker steamed ahead regardless.

'Blah blah Bosnia' amongst my colleagues was getting a bit boring, as it became increasingly clear to me that I was very much in the minority having never served in that theatre of operations. I decided that if there was any likelihood that this Kosovo operation might somehow kick off, I ought to try and do something about my Balkan virginity first. I devised a cunning plan.

Back in my old stamping ground, Bielefeld, the Army Prosecuting Authority was not the only ALS branch. Just up the road at Catterick Barracks was a department then known as Army Legal Aid. The name was misleading[31] because their mission was not to dish out money for soldiers' legal costs, but to provide individual soldiers legal advice on personal matters like divorce; in fact, the office was colloquially known as 'divorces for the forces'.

This was mostly undertaken in Germany, where there were thousands of soldiers with no easy access to British civilian lawyers but ALA's remit extended to all soldiers serving outside the UK and in order to service their need for legal advice the branch ran a programme of clinics, known as 'Legal Aid Bureaux'. Bosnia, where hundreds of British soldiers had been serving on six-month operational tours since 1995, was fertile ground for such business and a week-long bureau, in the form of a sort of legal roadshow conducted by an ALA captain took place there every two months throughout the year. The branch was run at that time by an old friend, Colonel Dick Austin, and I was able to persuade him that it would be a great idea to relieve one of his captains of yet another 'same old' trip to Bosnia and take on a legal aid bureau myself. I then ran the idea past the ARRC chief of staff[32] who agreed it would be good for me to 'get some mud on your boots', and it was fixed.

So, in mid-January 1999, having drawn a rucksack full of cold weather kit from the quartermaster and collected a handful of files from Bielefeld, I flew down to the NATO facility at Split, Croatia. The logistics for this were all set up by ALA's incomparable office manager, Tim Matthews, a retired Royal Artillery WO1, and I was met off the Hercules and driven for a pleasant overnight stay at the officers' transit accommodation in a villa overlooking the Adriatic. Dinner al fresco at Old Trogir was excellent and the weather was actually balmy after a very wintry northern Germany, so I was beginning to wonder what all the cold weather kit and fuss concerning Balkan operations was about.

The following morning, I was collected early in a Land Rover by the lance-corporal who would be my driver and companion for the next few days and we wound our way up out of the Croatian lowlands into the mountains. As we made our way up into Bosnia, it felt as if within a matter of a couple of hours we were in the Arctic and every few miles I was reaching over into my bag to find another layer to wear.

The Balkan microclimate is truly vicious, with roads which were clearly already poorly maintained now barely passable for snow and ice, in daytime temperatures struggling to better $-5°C$. There was certainly no question of getting any mud on my boots as everything was frozen solid but at least we were observing the spirit of the COS's comment, sleeping pretty rough in a number of different locations over the next few nights.

Everywhere we went I found Tim had laid the ground for my visits without a hitch, being greeted gratefully by adjutants who had arranged food and accommodation, an office to do business and an orderly queue of soldiers keen to offload anxieties from access to children to unaffordable NAAFI car loans to traffic offences.

Although the fighting in Bosnia was thankfully long since over, I soon began to see why an ALA captain who had made the trip several times had been happy to pass it up this time. Quite apart from the bitter weather, the environment was altogether bleak. The air over the towns and villages was heavily polluted from burning garbage, the once picturesque river valleys strewn with litter and burnt-out vehicles, and the graffiti-defiled villages themselves were largely in ruins, with minefield warnings round every corner, and the people wore pinched faces and rags. Most servicemen I know who have served in Northern Ireland, Iraq or Afghanistan seem to have at least something nostalgic to say about these places however rough a time they had, but I can't say the same about Bosnia. It's almost like Tolkien's[33] Mordor, a sinister place which you dread visiting, and once you leave you never look back.

Nevertheless, wherever I stopped, the army had somehow managed, as only an army can, to make itself adequately comfortable in the most unpromising circumstances, in places such as a bus station in historic Gorni Vakuf, which had seen vicious fighting. The most notorious location was the HQ at the Banja Luka Metal Factory, a sprawling camp, cosily located next to an ever-smouldering garbage heap, where officers and men alike slept in shipping containers, like refugees.

The days, of slow and hazardous road journeys and busy afternoons with clients, followed by nights spent vainly trying to get warm, passed quickly and I barely seemed to have arrived before we were wending our way back down to the coastal plain for the flight home.

It had been a really interesting visit, practising law with individual soldiers as clients for a change instead of the military chain of command, and learning something of their daily challenges while operating in a difficult and often depressing environment, particularly in the harshest of weather conditions. The enduring benefit, however, was that, as intended, the experience meant that at least I now had some idea what all the Bosnia veterans talked so much about. As it turned out, I had made the trip in the nick of time as I had barely returned to my office before developments in Kosovo took a serious turn for the worse and ARRC's deployment began to look very much more like a 'when' than an 'if'.

The incident in question – which I called the Franz Ferdinand moment, as the spark which started the fire – was an apparent massacre of forty-five Albanian Kosovars by Yugoslav forces in the Kosovo village of Racak on 15 January 1999. There can be no dispute about where and when all these victims died but the matter of how or why was the subject of heated debate at the time, and remains unresolved today, despite numerous inquiries.

The Yugoslav version of events was that all the victims were KLA insurgents who had opened fire on government forces which were in the area to suppress armed terrorist activity, and had been lawfully killed by them returning fire in self-defence. The fact that none of the bodies were in KLA uniforms was said to be because KLA survivors had later removed them from the bodies and replaced them with civilian clothes. The fact that most of the victims had been shot at close range was said to be because the KLA had shot them after they had been killed, to give an appearance of execution; in other words, the so-called 'massacre' was a set up by the KLA to provoke international action against Yugoslavia (which is, of course, exactly what happened).

The Kosovar story was that the Yugoslav forces, their faces masked by balaclavas, surrounded the village, which was only occupied by civilians, separated the men from the women and children, told them to run and then shot them from behind.

The 'genocide' genie was out of the bottle.

Which version of events you preferred depended, predictably, on your politics. Russia, in that rather hesitant interregnum between the Cold War and the (only slightly warmer) days of Putin remained firmly on the Serbs' side of the fence. The US view, expressed by President Clinton himself, who was if anything emboldened on the international scene by his domestic difficulties, was unequivocally to condemn the Yugoslavs. He was joined by the UK, glowing in the brave new world of Tony Blair and eager to stiffen the sinews of NATO if called upon, and so the inevitable 'something must be done' drumbeat grew louder by the day in Western Europe and beyond.

Consequently, although the pressure on the Yugoslavs to desist from alleged daily human rights violations against the Kosovar Albanians remained entirely diplomatic so far, it was increasingly leveraged by an undisguised threat of some sort of armed alternative, and the pace of planning and preparation at the ARRC accelerated tangibly.

By this time, after twelve months in my operational law billet, including a number of those delightful ARRC exercises, some refresher training at the NATO school at Oberammergau, a course at the US JAG school in Virginia and my chilly Bosnia trip, I was gaining confidence in the role. It did not take the brains of an archbishop to work out what I had always said about the legality of the use of force, and my view on that *ius ad bellum* question was, if anything, firmer than ever. Technically, even the threat of armed force breached the terms of the UN Charter but clearly such talk was not fashionable.

NATO's constitution requires the unanimous vote of all member states to embark on armed operations and so the problem of the 'legal landscape' was going to have to be tackled robustly by the 'hawks' if any such operation against Yugoslavia was actually going to happen.

That legal landscape looks a bit like this. Just as UK domestic law principally comprises the two elements of statute and the common law, so public international law also comprises two elements, which are treaty[34] law and customary international law. From time to time the customary law can tend to become a little 'untidy' and is then sometimes consolidated by treaties. All nations are bound by customary law, but only by those treaties which they have ratified. However, some treaties, or the majority of their contents, having been ratified by most nations, become so largely accepted over the years that they amount to customary law, meaning they are in effect universally binding, even upon those nations which have declined to ratify them.

The UN Charter, itself a treaty, quite clearly codifies pre-existing treaty and customary law on the vital matter of the resort to armed force against sovereign nations, but it has equally clearly failed to square the irreconcilable divergence between law and morality which inevitably arises from time to time in international affairs.

The silver bullet which was now being dangled before the hesitant to address this conundrum for Kosovo was an emerging doctrine called 'Humanitarian Intervention'.

In the first Gulf war of 1991 a US-led coalition acting under a UN mandate drove Saddam Hussein's shambolic Iraqi army out of Kuwait and Saddam then went on a killing spree against his own minority Kurdish community. The UNSCR authorizing the coalition's use of force against Iraq to liberate Kuwait was defunct by that stage as the job was done, and there was no self-defence basis on which the international community could rely in order to use force legally to protect the Kurds.

Nevertheless, the US proclaimed the view that, irrespective of the legal position, they retained a moral duty to continue to use force against the Iraqis in defence of the Kurds, an operation which continued in the form of an enforced 'no fly zone' for some years. This was the first modern example of the resort to armed force being justified on the basis of humanitarian intervention.

Audentis Fortuna Iuvat

In stark contrast, in 1994 the world just stood back and watched when nearly a million Tutsis perished at the hands of their Hutu tribal rivals in an internal massacre in Rwanda, because there was no legal basis for intervening and to do so would have infringed upon the sovereignty of the country.

The situation developing in Kosovo now presented the same bind for politicians between the demands of law and morality, but with events unfolding in Europe instead of deepest, darkest Africa there could be no question of turning a blind eye (itself perhaps a telling indicator of international notions of morality). According to the Albanian narrative there could be little argument against a moral obligation for the international community to try and help, but no government was going to risk taking military action without at least purported legal authority to do so. Thus, the British foreign secretary, Robin Cook[35] stated, after the event: 'In international law, in exceptional circumstances and to avoid a humanitarian catastrophe, military action can be taken and it is on that legal basis that military action was taken.'

However much he and many others might have wished it were so, this was simply incorrect; humanitarian intervention may be a moral basis but it is *not* a legal one. The principal argument to the contrary is that humanitarian intervention had developed to become a part of customary international law. The inconvenient truth is that the way customary international law is established can only be by means of 'state practice'; in short, the conduct in question has been repeated over a substantial period and become generally accepted, in particular by legal experts in the field, as demonstrated by judicial decisions.[36] Arguably, neither of those prerequisites applies to establish armed humanitarian intervention as a matter of customary law even today, and it certainly did not in 1999.

Fortunately for those advocates of such intervention on the moral basis of protecting people's human rights, the average voter, at least in the developed world, nowadays has quite a clear idea of the meaning of the term 'human rights' but very little idea about international law. Thus, for example, when Bashar al-Assad decides to use banned chemical weapons against Syrian insurgents and Donald Trump decides to punish him by launching a cruise missile strike against his airfields, the vast majority of people assume that must be legally OK, but it is not. If the US was under threat from those chemical weapons, it would be legally entitled to respond in self-defence, but it was not and never has been under any such threat.[37]

This legal limitation has proved unwelcome for the US more than once, hence the 'Bush doctrine' well before the Trump presidency, purportedly extending the meaning of acting in self-defence to 'pre-emptive' strikes, against even ideological threats as well as military ones. Had anybody challenged Trump over the action against the Assad regime, that doctrine would no doubt have been cited as the legal authority but the use of chemical weapons is so universally abhorred that nobody really even bothered to ask the question.

Along with other world affairs, the US was keen to dominate international law but the fact that George. W. purported single-handedly to adjust international law to suit US interests did not enable him to do so.[38] However, it is reasonable to ask, 'Well then, what is the international community supposed to do when such an appalling weapon is unlawfully used?'

One answer today is that since 2002 there has been a legal forum in the Hague for dealing with war crimes; it is called the International Criminal Court.[39] The ICC is far from the perfect solution and does not offer the dramatic political grandstand of an immediate kinetic strike but it does provide for considered due process against clearly identified defendants. That is called the 'rule of law', which is how the West is supposed to do business, as it repeatedly reminds its opponents, and the UN has rightly restricted the lawful resort to the use of armed force to two very specific circumstances, as above, extending which (for example, to using it as 'punishment') is to tread an extremely slippery slope.

To put this another way, two wrongs do not make a right, so where you (apparently) have Yugoslav government forces acting repeatedly in breach of international human rights law, it cannot be right for other nations who happen to be mightier than Yugoslavia to respond by acting in breach of another law, the *ius ad bellum*, to punish them. Under the rule of law, surely, we do not respond to perceived shortcomings in the law by disobeying it like the 'bad guys'; we work within it and try to persuade others to do so, or if necessary, try to change it peaceably, don't we?

Well, that's what I thought anyway, but I guess where there's a clash between the law and realpolitik there can be only one winner, otherwise Jesus would probably have died in his bed and Donald Trump could never re-enter politics. The credibility of NATO, celebrating its 50th anniversary that very same year, was at stake here, particularly given ongoing controversy over its raison d'être following the end of the Cold

War, and planning had now reached a stage whereby the momentum for military action was practically unstoppable.

Viscerally hostile to Serbia, Madeleine Albright led the charge, saying of the Serbs, 'They need some bombing, and that's what they're going to get.' If the situation during the previous year could be compared to a parachutist's descent, it had now clearly gone from steady whilst intermittently buffeted – to ground rush.

The endgame for diplomacy was being played out near Paris at the Palais de Rambouillet, in an attempt by the third party 'Contact Group' of nations to repeat the effect of the Dayton agreement which had finally brought the war in Bosnia to an end only a few years earlier. The Yugoslavs and the Kosovar Albanians had been brought together in the vain hope of brokering a settlement of their differences. Perhaps the biggest miscalculation made by the group in hoping for a similar outcome to Dayton was the importance of Kosovo to both protagonists.

For Serbia, Kosovo was far more important both historically and symbolically than Bosnia and for the Kosovar Albanians it represented the only show in town if the dream of a 'Greater Albania' was ever to be realized. Thus, unless the Yugoslav side could be satisfied that the status of the province as an enduring part of their sovereign territory was guaranteed, they were never going to sign up. As for the Kosovar side, they were very happy to consolidate their perceived perch on the moral high ground by signing what was offered. They could not lose, because if the Serbs declined to sign, they would be bombed into submission and if they did sign Kosovo would sooner or later become independent, as the Albanians wanted.

There was another passage in the proposed terms, reminiscent once again of the 1914 Austro-Hungarian ultimatum to Serbia, which was obviously unacceptable to them. The Contact Group's plan was for a NATO formation on the ground to oversee a peaceful settlement in Kosovo; so far so good, but it went on to propose that NATO would also have the right for complete freedom of movement and action throughout all Yugoslav territory. Clearly this was totally unacceptable to the Yugoslav negotiators, and understandably so. The question is: how could such an unnecessary condition find its way into the text? Henry Kissinger[40] thought the answer was clear; it was 'a provocation – an excuse to start bombing'.

It seems doubtful that even the most hawkish proponents of military action would have wanted it to endure for longer than absolutely necessary to bring Milosevic to heel, but their eagerness to secure the essential consensus of reluctant NATO members for any sort of military action presented a dilemma which proved costly. The prospect of an opposed invasion of a relatively well-armed Yugoslavia by NATO on the ground was almost guaranteed to bring dissent from member states such as Greece[41] in the North Atlantic Council.[42]

Therefore, in order to sell the plan of a strictly aerial campaign, NATO had to declare publicly that in no circumstances would this lead to military action on the ground. In Belgrade this message was music to Milosevic's ears as he undoubtedly concluded that he just had to face down the air campaign for long enough for NATO's resolve to collapse, and with no risk of escalation into an invasion – he had won.

Irrespective of all that top-level business, things were getting serious back at HQ ARRC too. Spies had already been dispatched in various guises to gather as much intelligence on the ground down south as possible and more overtly we were looking in detail at our role in forthcoming events. That was actually the relatively easy bit, and our orders from SACEUR laid it out. The ARRC was to deploy a force of approximately 30,000 soldiers into the Kosovo region, prepared to enter the province on orders to secure and maintain peace and security, hopefully under UN auspices, until such time as a civilian administration, again probably a UN mission, could safely take over pending a permanent settlement of the status of the province. The structure of the force, which after much agonizing became christened KFOR for Kosovo Force, would be made up of national formations from the UK, US, France, Germany (a first since the Second World War) and Italy.

Until the previous year many of us in Rheindahlen had never even heard of Kosovo, let alone its capital city, Pristina and equally we had only a vague notion of the geography of the rest of the southern Balkan region. What we did now learn rapidly was that the only options for our entry into Kosovo on the ground would be from Albania to the east or FYROM to the south.

Albania was only slowly emerging from an almost mediaeval forty-year era under the regime of the bizarre Communist dictator Enver Hoxha. Geographically it was equally unpromising, with terrible infrastructure and a mountainous border with Kosovo which was perfect for KLA insurgent operations but not for large-scale conventional forces. FYROM, on the other hand, despite also only recently emerging from the Eastern bloc, was not only NATO friendly, as a PfP (NATO Partnership

Audentis Fortuna Iuvat

for Peace) nation, but also relatively developed, with good links to the Greek port of Thessaloniki and easier access to Kosovo itself.

So, the plan was that we would make Skopje, the capital of FYROM, our HQ, with something called Rear Support Command at Thessaloniki[43] as the logistic command centre for anything joining us by sea, and JHQ Rheindahlen as rear HQ.

While the spies were doing their spying north of the border in Kosovo, various senior ARRC officers were reconnoitring FYROM for suitable locations for the NATO formation, including HQ KFOR. They reported back sometime in February and I clearly recall the Command Group[44] meeting at which the options were presented to COMARRC.

'So, what have you got for us, Andrew?' asked the general of the recce commander.

'There are two options for HQ KFOR in Skopje, General; first, the Hotel Continental looks promising. It could comfortably accommodate the numbers we need, it's in quite a good location, easily secured, good comms, catering, etc.'

This was accompanied by a few slides of a twelve-storey Soviet 1960s-style tower block which, although architecturally pretty offensive, seemed otherwise OK for a couple of months, with a reasonable bar and catering downstairs. The atmosphere in the room was one of pleasant surprise at this prospect.

Deployment for an open-ended commitment in the field is understandably seen as a mixed blessing among very senior officers. Having had their excitement, reached their promotion ceiling and already earnt their medals, some had until recent months been looking forward to retiring peacefully to Wiltshire in the near future. I could sense in the meeting an immediate mental jockeying for position among brigadiers, visualizing single bedrooms with colour TV, mini bars, room service and en suite facilities.

However, turning to the general for his reaction, faces immediately fell somewhat. He was one of the few people anybody knew who was said to have actually quite liked living at the Banja Luka Metal Factory when he was in Bosnia. Now he was looking distinctly sceptical, and sure enough … harrumph!

'And the second option?'

The answer was inevitably what we ended up with, a semi-derelict former factory, the Gazela Shoe Factory, later dubbed by our ever-inventive soldiers the 'Godzilla shit factory'. The general was absolutely right, of course: comfy though the hotel might have been, it lacked the office space, perimeter security, vehicle hard standing and flexibility of Gazela, but above all it just wouldn't 'look right' for a NATO corps HQ engaged in a major operation to be checking in[45] to a hotel.[46]

The month of March was a blur. The Rambouillet process, having already been extended into late February, was accorded one further month, until 23 March but was still getting nowhere fast. I took a slow, noisy Hercules ride from RAF Bruggen[47] to Skopje with other HQ 'key leaders' for our own familiarization with the deployed HQ, as the realization dawned on us that after all the uncertainty and detailed preparation of the last twelve months and despite my thoughts on legality, this was really going to happen after all.

On arrival there was yet another planning conference, at which most of us met for the first time the commanders of the major formations which would make up KFOR: the UK 4th Armoured Brigade's patrician Brigadier Bill Rollo, the lofty French General Valentin, complete with classic Gallic profile of which De Gaulle would have been proud, and the charming General John Craddock of the US 1st Infantry Division (the 'Big Red One').[48] Last but not least, the Italian formation commander was a totally bald-headed brigadier, who again seemed thoroughly charming but spoke not one word of English, relying entirely on an extremely competent bilingual Italian lieutenant-colonel for his contribution to business with ARRC HQ. Nobody seemed to know the brigadier's name but his unit was proudly entitled the Garibaldi Brigade, which was inevitably rechristened by our soldiers the 'Barry Baldy Brigade' in his honour.

On 19 March, back in Germany, we celebrated the accession to NATO of three new member states, Poland, Hungary[49] and the Czech Republic. This was marked with a modest parade and a not so modest party in the mess at which we were royally entertained by each of our new allies, with vodka, Bull's Blood, and Budvar flowing freely; you could almost have forgotten that there was about to be 'a war on'.

During the preceding couple of weeks, I had been laying out my kit for departure in my spare bedroom, obsessively adding and subtracting. Now it would just have to do, as we were on our way. The office material had already been dispatched and our pitch in the bowels of the shoe factory staked out during the recce visit. I would be accompanied by the ever-cheerful Bart Haverman the Dutchman, while the office in Rear would be manned initially by Major Richard Batty, a UK ALS colleague who had been posted in and was due to arrive any day soon.

As we waited outside the 'Big House' for the bus to take us out to Bruggen, there were a lot of nervous faces and I noticed a number of colleagues who appeared suddenly to have become smokers. This was no routine six-month operational deployment into a steady-state established theatre; we had no idea how it was going to play out or how long we would be away.

At least things started off well because I found I was amongst a fortunate number going to war in a Queen's flight 'whisper Jet' borrowed from Northolt instead of the usual Herc', complete with uniformed stewards serving drinks.[50]

It promised to be the last real comfort for some months; the Shoe Factory awaited.

Chapter 3

The Front-line Factory

When we touched down at Petrovac airport, Skopje, most of us in the ARRC knew even less about the country which we would call home for the foreseeable future than we did about Kosovo. Formerly the poorest republic in the federated Yugoslavia, FYROM gained independence bloodlessly following an overwhelming referendum mandate in 1991. About two-thirds the size of Switzerland, with a population in the region of two million, most Macedonians are Christian but a quarter of the population is ethnic Albanian.

Eighty per cent of Skopje was destroyed by an earthquake in July 1963. This was particularly bad timing as the rebuilding of the city during the ensuing years coincided with the era of brutalist Soviet architecture, so it is really not a pretty sight. The infrastructure was poor and both traffic and pollution heavy, particularly in our part of town, which was hardly Belgravia.

The shoe factory had been a going concern until very shortly before our arrival, an event which delighted its owner, whose rent from NATO comfortably exceeded his profits from making uncomfortable shoes. Our delightful Italian deputy commander was not impressed, however, and was seldom seen. Rumour had it that he had taken one look at the premises and declared, 'I not living in thees sheet 'ole,' before returning to Rome, where he spent the majority of the next few weeks. Nobody blamed him for this, as his role in the field would have been frustratingly limited, although we did miss the coffee in his outer office.

The advance party had worked tirelessly to remove heavy manufacturing plant from the building to make way for our accommodation but this work was still in progress when we arrived. For the first few weeks, apart from COMARRC, who sensibly elected to sleep in his office, we were living on an extremely grimy factory floor, with minimal privacy and ablutions, using a hot water system reinvented by an enterprising Pioneer warrant officer, probably last used in the Crimean War. Things did improve, however, as an impressively energetic project saw the construction of rows of two-man dormitory cubicles, rapidly dubbed 'veal crates'. These reminded me of boarding school but they were in fact quite civilized, so we now had a bit of comfort, good food, laundry service and even a bar, with Jacko maintaining the old-fashioned view that even, or perhaps especially, in uncertain times, man cannot live by bread alone.

The way the HQ swung into action to make day-to-day living work so well was truly impressive, but the first couple of weeks were extremely tense for everybody. The Rambouillet process finally ground to a halt within days of our arrival, with only the prospect of the NATO air campaign against Yugoslavia remaining on the table. Our formation within FYROM was almost entirely command and logistic, and if the Yugoslavs had decided to risk taking us on militarily as Milosevic had threatened to do, we would have been in trouble.

We were well within Serb artillery range and our defence was rudimentary: soldiers with rifles, officers with pistols, some basic air defence equipment at the airfields and virtually nothing in the way of tanks, artillery or local air defence. Opposing us, should they choose, were substantial tank formations with Soviet kit which was old but still pretty effective when unopposed, heliborne special forces, and Russian MiGs at Pristina airport, one minute's flying time away. A single NATO combat air patrol (CAP) fighter jet was supposed to be overhead at all times to provide reassurance but even that was weather dependant.

In common with most factories built behind the Iron Curtain during the Cold War we did at least have a proper underground shelter, a distinct advantage over any hotel, although it was pretty basic and nobody fancied having to spend much time down there. Weapons and ammunition were issued to all, in my case for the first time since all those years ago in Ireland, and the factory windows were taped up, reminding me of pictures of London in the blitz.

When the Rambouillet talks finally collapsed on 23 March the bombing campaign began immediately.

The general remarked to the command group that evening: 'Gentlemen, this may not seem much like the Duchess of Richmond's Ball[1] but it could be our "Night before Waterloo".'

You didn't need to be a historian for that reference to send you to bed a little nervous.

Throughout NATO's time on their soil the FYROM government was conflicted about how to regard us. On the one hand we were clearly seen as a hugely valuable cash cow, to be exploited financially at every turn in return for the use of strategically essential real estate scattered throughout the north of their country. The downside for them was that having escaped the clutches of the post-communist Yugoslav federation without a drop of blood being spilt, unlike their near neighbours Bosnia and Croatia, their warmth towards us might ultimately bring about dire consequences if the NATO operation all went wrong and Milosevic decided to come and seek revenge.

This paranoia came to a head within twenty-four hours of the bombing beginning, when a large, angry mob of Milosevic's sympathizers, many of them bussed in across the border from Serbia, besieged the US, British and German embassies, nearly provoking an armed response from a US unit already deployed in country. In the end the incident was dealt with by the FYROM riot police, but not before I had been called upon to brief our perimeter defenders on their rules of engagement, as we were rumoured to be the next target, which fortunately did not transpire. However, the British ambassador and his family were hastily evacuated from their residence to spend an uncomfortable night as our guests, before repatriation to London, and General Jackson was summoned by a panic-stricken FYROM government to convince them that NATO was going to maintain control.

The issue of rules of engagement was a legal problem which I had identified well before we deployed, and continued to wrestle with throughout our time in FYROM. ROE are a compendium of rules issued to armed forces on an operation by air, land or sea, setting out the permissions or limitations applied to their movements and use of force at all stages of the operation. Most nations' armed forces' operations are controlled by ROE, which have three components: policy, military operational requirements, and the law. Contrary to popular misconception, ROE are not pure law, but they must be lawful,[2] and providing a soldier complies with his ROE, he will be acting lawfully.[3]

When nations contribute troops to a NATO operation, they are all bound by the ROE issued by NATO for that operation. In this way allied commanders are able to deploy troops under their command from a variety of different nations knowing they are all 'singing from the same song sheet' instead of each following different national rules.[4] In the absence of any such ROE being issued by NATO, the troop-contributing

The Front-line Factory

nations can only rely on their own national rules, so in FYROM in March 1999 you would have at least five different nations each bound by different rules, clearly a handicap for COMARRC.

All NATO operational plans contain an ROE annexe, but as we prepared to deploy I had become increasingly concerned that NATO had issued us no rules for FYROM. The compilation of NATO ROE in SHAPE at that time was apparently entirely controlled by a rather ferocious female Canadian legal lieutenant-colonel, who persistently stonewalled my demands, which was embarrassing for me every time the general asked me, 'How are we doing with those ROE?'

By the time we deployed we were no further ahead, and the last straw for me came one afternoon when I was being driven in a Land Rover to a meeting in Skopje and narrowly avoided an accident while swerving to avoid rocks being thrown at us by Serb sympathizers. Arriving slightly shaken back at my 'office', I fired off another furious demand, and finally received a reply: 'There will be no NATO ROE for FYROM. You are in a "non-hostile" environment, for which there is no requirement for NATO to issue ROE.'

I replied to the effect that it might not seem hostile to people sitting back comfortably in Belgium, but with rioting, stoning, a French APC[5] set on fire with the crew having to be rescued at gunpoint, not to mention potential attack from north of the border, it felt pretty damn hostile to us. The problem, reading between the lines, was that NATO ROE have to be signed off unanimously by the NAC, who had been totally preoccupied with ROE for the air campaign, and then for the land peacekeeping operation in Kosovo which they expected to be imminent, so our time in FYROM was merely an afterthought which NATO had calculated would only last for a week or two at most. The bottom line was that we would just have to 'suck it up', as our transatlantic chums say.

I had learnt a while ago that while I was in a NATO appointment, there was effectively no such thing as UK national 'reach back' for my office to rely on[6] and I either had to work things out for myself or try and persuade somebody at the SHAPE legal office to help me or at least to see my point of view when I had a problem. Fortunately, I had a good ALS friend, Nigel Jones, working there, but as a very young and even more junior lieutenant-colonel than me, his experience and authority were no greater than mine just because he happened to be working in a higher HQ in the NATO chain of command.

His boss, the senior lawyer at SHAPE, was inevitably American, at that time a civilian who was close to retirement and apparently not as engaged as you might hope at a time of crisis like this. Matters became even more complicated when we deployed, because at that point the position of the ARRC itself moved within the same chain of command to come under NATO's HQ AFSouth (Armed Forces South), based in Naples and commanded by US Admiral Jim Ellis, who in turn reported to SACEUR at SHAPE. The chief lawyer in Naples was also American, a JAG Corps colonel, so he became my 'one up' in the legal chain.

I had spent a month during the summer of 1998 at the US JAG Corps training establishment in Charlottesville, Virginia on a Law of War (*sic*) workshop (where, funny old thing, the scenario used for our exercises was 'Op Balkan Storm', a US invasion of Kosovo from Albania). This had been instructive in many ways, not least because I learnt that not only are Great Britain and the USA 'two great nations separated by a common language'[7] but also that their respective military legal establishments interpret the law of armed conflict quite differently in many respects. So at least I was forewarned and forearmed, but on a number of issues during this operation I found the combination of those discrepancies and the apparent lack of urgency further up the chain of command and away from the front line desperately frustrating. Indeed, I rapidly came to understand one of the golden rules of military operations: everybody hates their higher headquarters.

It seemed every one of the legal 'building blocks' for this sort of deployment foreseen by international law was missing. First, the *ius ad bellum*, secondly the ROE, and thirdly the legal status of 'visiting forces'.

Shortly after its formation NATO implemented a 'status of forces agreement',[8] or SOFA which is a treaty setting out the legal regime applicable to personnel of member states operating on duty within the territorial legal jurisdiction of other member states. The classic example of this SOFA, and its later 'supplementary agreement' in action, is its application to British and US troops in Germany throughout the Cold War (that was the jurisdiction for court-martial business back in Bielefeld in my previous job). Such agreements are invariably negotiated when, for example, nations send troops overseas on peacekeeping missions, and indeed the UN has its own model SOFA specifically designed as a template, to be adapted and applied appropriately on UN-mandated operations.

A SOFA's most practically important provisions cover such matters as criminal jurisdiction over visiting forces personnel alleged to have committed crimes in the host nation's territory, tax arrangements for visiting forces and the customs liabilities to which they may or may not be subjected for the goods and kit associated with their mission which they bring in and out of that country.

Such legal provisions are probably even more important in most operations than ROE, because although soldiers may never be forced to open fire and then justify their actions, they will inevitably import weapons, vehicles and food, and probably even unknowingly sometimes commit offences against local law, so they need to know where they stand.

COMARRC was well aware of all this business, not least following his Bosnia experience and one day in Skopje he specifically asked me: 'Who has jurisdiction over a military driver who gets drunk and kills a Macedonian child?'[9]

A perfectly reasonable question, to which, through no fault of my own the only answer I could provide was that infuriating lawyer's fall-back, 'It depends'.

It should have been easy, because FYROM was a PfP nation, and the PfP had its own SOFA which was pretty much identical to the NATO SOFA. The problem was that certain NATO nations had not yet ratified the PfP Treaty, amongst whom was, guess who ... the UK, so the treaty, including its SOFA, was inapplicable and non-binding between FYROM and the UK. In the absence of any other legally binding status, that meant that all UK personnel deployed as members of KFOR were, for legal purposes ... tourists. They had no more right to import or export weapons, vehicles, foodstuffs or anything else, let alone expect to be protected under UK law should they be arrested, than Mrs Miggins on her Thompsons all-inclusive package holiday.[10]

It was not just the boss who would ask me questions like this from time to time and when I told people that was their status, they thought I was kidding. Who can blame them – it was a pretty unbelievable failure of our FCO bureaucracy which was not rectified until May that year, and only then through persistent pressure starting at my level.

The way round this which was negotiated between NATO and FYROM was that the relevant issues would be dealt with under a bilateral treaty known as the 'Basic Agreement', effectively bypassing the PfP arrangements, comprising ten different annexes, from crime to tax with everything else in between. This was agreed verbally by FYROM, which was effectively meaningless (because you try quoting that verbal agreement to Mr Macedonian customs officer when you are trying to bring an artic' full of refrigerated food in from Bulgaria), but had to be formalized by a diplomatic 'exchange of letters', which was like the proverbial cheque in the post. The whole deal was an utterly Byzantine mess, a perfect storm of NATO improvisation, vestigial Soviet-style bureaucracy, naked FYROM economic opportunism and political paranoia.

To address these matters there was a weekly meeting at the FYROM MoD of a so-called 'committee of experts', who were supposed to be the ministers with all the relevant portfolios, such as defence, foreign affairs, police, agriculture, home affairs etc. but eventually every minister from arts to zoology turned up, seeing the forum as a sort of bazaar at which NATO funds were to be extorted on a never-ending list of pretexts. NATO's chief representative was the extremely affable and long-suffering Brigadier David Montgomery, supported by various staff officers like me.

At every one of these meetings, without fail, we were overwhelmed by lengthy diatribes via interpreter on a wide variety of themes, all seemingly aimed at amending unilaterally any provisions of the agreement seen as preventing the government of FYROM receiving NATO money. In a time when mobile phones were relatively novel, especially in less-developed countries, they were also clearly an important status symbol, only augmenting the babble with incessant irritating musical ring tones. I seem to recall 'William Tell' was a Skopje favourite.

The agreement called for NATO to buy food locally 'where possible', but apart from excellent wine-producing grapes, FYROM didn't seem to grow much at all, so usually it wasn't 'possible' and we had to import most of the needs of the thousands of troops in country. To add insult to injury as far as the locals were concerned, the agreement exempted NATO from paying import duties for these foodstuffs. Inevitably customs officers deliberately tried to confuse these rules, so we were endlessly having to fend off attempts to levy unlawful import duties, in order to get trucks across the border into the country before the food went off.

We were also entitled under the agreement to free use of various barrack facilities. The relevant ministry refused to accept this and wanted to charge ridiculous rates of rent. NATO in turn quite rightly refused, but it meant many soldiers living in unnecessarily inadequate or uncomfortable accommodation under canvas for many weeks, while the barracks sat empty.

The agreement provided for 'sending state' jurisdiction in cases where soldiers committed traffic offences, but again NATO officers repeatedly found themselves at local police stations trying to explain this to FYROM police officers who were intent on dealing with such matters themselves.

FYROM were not all to blame; they sometimes had a point. If Brussels had been a bit more proactive in responding to our repeated requests to deal with the simple exchange of letters, albeit via the tedious command chain of both AFSouth and SHAPE, a lot of this nonsense could have been resolved early on, much improving relations between visitors and hosts.

I recall spending a very long Friday evening at my desk after one of these exhausting and useless 'experts' meetings, setting out the issues to AFSouth legal branch in several pages of email and requesting assistance, yet again. This was still early on, so not only was I seriously concerned about these potentially strategic legal deficiencies for which I had to answer to my boss, but like everyone else at the HQ the possibility of an imminent attack from the north was always on my mind. We all had our professional doubts and challenges and our more private fears but I think without exception we felt 'up to our arse in alligators' and in need of support.

I received a prompt but succinct reply from Chief Legal in sunny Naples the very next morning. This is not verbatim, but pretty close:

> Hi Jim. Thanks for your message. You're doing a great job down there and you obviously have a real good grip on all the issues. We really appreciate that and we're here to support you all the way. My sister's here visiting me from the States right now so I'm off for the day taking her to lunch. We'll get right back to you after the weekend.[11]

I was speechless with fury, and after allowing myself a few minutes to calm down, I was banging on the chief of staff's door. When I showed him the message his language was unrepeatable, but we both knew there was no point in pursuing that conversation any further.

Nevertheless, we ploughed on with our business of trying to be courteous and honest partners with our host nation, so that whilst trying not to be ripped off we also paid our way.

A time-honoured aspect of this sort of relationship was the damage which a powerful house guest like NATO can do to the infrastructure of an underdeveloped host, for example with large tracked vehicles on cheaply built roads. If the 'coalition of the willing' which briefly occupied parts of oil-rich Saudi Arabia in 1991 was economically a pimple on an elephant, NATO's deployment in FYROM in 1999 was an elephant squishing an impoverished pimple, at some risk to the latter.

So, we set up a claims office under our NATO Military Liaison Team to compensate local citizens and businesses for loss or damage caused by NATO in the course of operations, exercises or just transiting through the country. For this we had an up-to-date template, based on the Bosnia model and I was really grateful to my SHAPE colleagues for their help in setting things up.[12] We had a non-contentious claims system for dealing with damages caused by individual national forces or NATO as a whole, and a tribunal to determine contested matters, together with checks and balances against the inevitable double-tap claims, and we hired a local lawyer to advise on Macedonian law and quantum of damages.

Not surprisingly, when word of this organization got out it was a great hit, with claims flooding in. They ranged from companies claiming for loss of income from trade with Serbia because of the bombing and the closed border (inadmissible) to farmers' claims for pigs miscarrying due to low-flying helicopters, known as PTSD or 'Pigs Traumatic Stress Disorder' (sometimes admissible, sometimes just entertaining). Although at times we were less than sympathetic, we could understand the claimants' point of view.

The whole country was already politically unstable due to ethnic friction between the Slavic majority and the growing Albanian minority but what happened next threatened to overwhelm them.

Milosevic had not survived the Bosnian war just by good fortune; he was a shrewd political operator and, realizing that following through on a military threat against the might of NATO in FYROM was never going to end well for him, he adopted a much smarter approach altogether. The whole rationale for the NATO air campaign in Kosovo and the rest of Serbia was of course to alleviate the human rights, indeed apparently genocidal, abuses against the Kosovar Albanians. However, as soon as the bombing began there was a massive flood[13] of Albanian Kosovar refugees out of Kosovo, some into Albania, but principally into FYROM. This, although partly spontaneous, was largely deliberately engineered by the Serb national forces in Kosovo.

For Milosevic this was a win, win, win. You purged Kosovo of the Albanians, which was always a good thing, you showed the world that NATO's whole strategy was deeply flawed by punishing the terrified Albanians instead of saving them which it claimed to be doing, and you threatened to ruin the economy and demography of FYROM which could not possibly feed and accommodate all these unwelcome ethnic strangers even if it had wanted to, which it didn't. Better still, FYROM might even decide the solution would be to throw NATO out, thereby pulling the rug from under the whole operation and drawing FYROM back to cooperating with the FRY. All this was conveniently assisted by the Greeks, who, despite their government's unpopular official position, were increasingly supportive of the Serbs.[14]

NATO now also found itself facing increasing demands from the international NGO community to suspend the air campaign. The purpose of this proposal was to permit safe passage within Kosovo for humanitarian relief missions to assist the refugees and internally displaced civilians on the ground, the vast majority of whom were of course from the Kosovar Albanian community whom we were trying to help. This was firmly rejected by NATO, which, probably correctly, concluded that any such temporary 'cease-fire' was likely to prove irreversible, given the jitters which were already evident amongst some member states. I could not help smiling ruefully at this rationale. To recap, the so-called 'legal justification' for the military operation was 'humanitarian intervention' but now that same operation must not be jeopardized by, yes, you've got it ... the intervention of the humanitarians! As Margaret Thatcher said with understandable acidity at her last cabinet meeting: 'It's a funny old world.'

Overnight, the ARRC in FYROM was forced to adjust from expectant bystander, as the air campaign dragged on and on with no sign of Yugoslav capitulation, to refugee management on a massive scale. Air traffic in and out of Petrovac went from being Croydon airfield 1938 to London Heathrow 1999 within a matter of days as fleets of aircraft importing food, tentage, bedding and medical supplies from non-governmental organizations and nations in all corners of the globe began to arrive.

Fortunately, logistics was something we were really good at and a combination of a massive practical effort on the ground[15] and daily diplomacy by COMARRC soon had the situation more or less under control and the collective furrowed brows of the FYROM politicians once again adequately soothed.

Nevertheless, this did nothing to calm our jitters, with speculation that if Milosevic did manage to hold on until winter, a massive humanitarian disaster in the snow-covered mountain refugee camps was inevitable. Speculation mounted about the need to consider going in on the ground after all, and sooner rather than later, in order to avoid such an outcome.

Not long after my arrival in theatre I discovered that I was not the only UK ALS officer there, as two of my colleagues had arrived as legal advisers in the main British formations, Captains Elliot Glover with 4th Armoured Brigade, and Jo Bowen with 101 Logistics Brigade.[16] I thought it might be good for the morale of all three of us to meet up, and having found out they were both together for the time being at the 101 Brigade HQ a few miles east of Skopje, I took a trip out there.

My visit coincided with an alarming intelligence report of a possible Serb special forces attack against this lightly armed location, and the atmosphere was tense. As we sat in the warm spring sunshine, Elliot was loading his pistol, hands a little shaky. Jo had another reason for nervousness, having had a run-in with the brigade commander within days of taking up her appointment.

A medical unit, properly marked with the red cross on the roof, had been set up right next to brigade HQ. Jo had quite rightly pointed out that, although not strictly illegal, this was a very bad idea. Quite apart from the risk to patients and staff as collateral casualties should an attack be launched against the HQ, which was a perfectly lawful military target, the use of the red cross could lead to allegations that it had been deliberately displayed to protect the HQ from attack by disguising it all as a field hospital. Such a deception, if determined to be deliberate, would be an unlawful act of perfidy.

No legal advice had been sought before this was all set up but when she realized what had happened, Jo had courageously come forward and strongly advised that the two establishments must not be co-located and one or other would have to move. The brigadier was not happy, but the medical unit was eventually moved and the very junior Jo earned the respect she deserved.

The Front-line Factory

Although the special forces threat never materialized in FYROM, we felt very close to the action, with many nights in Skopje punctuated by the sounds of the bombing to the north.[17] I was asked if we could task our own special forces in the hills overlooking the Kosovo border to laser 'paint' targets for 'smart' bombing, but one of the conditions of our presence in FYROM was that NATO should not engage in any offensive military action from its territory or airspace.[18] The proposal would clearly have been a 'hostile act' and thus a clear breach of the restriction, and I advised accordingly.

Judging by the fast-jet air traffic overhead every day, which was obviously more than just our defensive CAP, somebody seemed to have forgotten the blanket prohibition on offensive action. One morning at the commander's 8 am 'prayers' we all instinctively ducked as the roar of a jet engine coming in from the west nearly took the roof off the shoe factory. This was becoming ridiculous, and having dusted ourselves off, some extremely grumpy inquiries were made as to who the hell was responsible. It turned out to be a US cruise missile headed for Pristina, not only rather too close for comfort but a very clear infringement.

On another occasion I was woken at about 2 am by an enormous explosion which again shook the building; clearly the long-dreaded artillery barrage was finally incoming. I leapt from my bed, clenching my buttocks and, grabbing tin hat and body armour, hurtled like a greased racing-snake for the shelter, braced for the next rounds. My enormous relief as minutes ticked by and nothing else happened was mixed with incomprehension, because with the exception of a handful of others, nobody else even seemed to be awake, let alone lurking in the basement.

After a few minutes our nervous little huddle decided that whatever had gone bang in the night, it did not appear to be the Yugoslav Army, so, removing our helmets, we slunk sheepishly back to bed, whistling softly and trying to look nonchalant for the benefit of anyone we might bump into. The next morning, I was relieved to find that I was not going crazy after all because there was much speculation about the night's disturbance as we assembled for 'prayers', although to my amazement most people had not heard a thing, and slept right through it. It turned out that the bang was not my imagination but an earthquake, which despite the volume was a single tremor, and amazingly had done no noticeable damage.

Morning prayers was everyone's daily opportunity for a reality check, chaired by the commander and comprising an audience of about twenty-five officers of whom some invariably had a speaking role, such as G2 Int, who always kicked off with the met' report followed by a mixture of open and classified material about what was supposedly happening or likely to happen next, then G3 Ops, G4 Logistics, G5 Plans, Media Ops and several others. Legal was optional, so I tried to strike a balance between showing we were earning our pay by providing a brief update, and avoiding wasting busy people's time with technical legal business causing eyes to glaze over.

Despite his slightly fearsome reputation, General Jackson usually maintained a very relaxed style amongst his staff, even during times which must have been extremely taxing, not least trying to keep the lid on relations with the host government, and General Ridgway's light touch complemented him well. This rubbed off, so that there was often a refreshing element of humour in the proceedings,[19] but you could tell when matters were getting really serious, as the rank of the slide show operator would shoot up from corporal to brigadier.

Some element of levity was important because we all needed an antidote to the, often ridiculous, propaganda put out by NATO[20] through the media about, for example, hordes of deserting Yugoslav soldiers,[21] the number of Yugoslav tanks destroyed and Yugoslav soldiers abusing Kosovars in 'rape camps' (nobody even knew what one of those was). Some of it was quite funny, but some so ludicrous as to be embarrassing for us on the ground, where we had a very clear picture of what was being portrayed rather differently to the wider world.

I recall General Ridgway's wise words at the time: 'When you see what rubbish is sometimes talked about matters which you know about, just imagine how much rubbish is also being talked about the stuff you don't.' To be fair, the Serb propaganda was invariably a guinea a minute too!

The other event which took place some mornings and also demanded a large pinch of salt was the video conference for all the appropriate NATO formation HQs, usually chaired by Wes Clark at SHAPE. Wes didn't start off with much of a sense of humour but as the days of bombing turned to weeks with no sign of the desired effect despite the carnage allegedly being unleashed, he became visibly tetchier. This came to a head one morning when he subjected the audience to a ten-minute haranguing which was his version of a call to arms. We were threatened with 'total war, glass in the Coca-Cola, dead babies, no leave' and a variety of other random horrors, for which we should prepare by adopting the 'spirit of the bayonet'.

The Front-line Factory

Wes addressed Admiral Ellis himself at AFSouth: 'Do you understand the spirit of the bayonet, Jim?'

Of course, sailors and bayonets are strangers really – maybe the 'spirit of the cutlass' would have worked better – and the admiral looked distinctly uncomfortable, but felt obliged to mumble, 'Oh sure, General.'

We all emerged at the end of this tirade rather shaken, as if we had just been addressed by Dr Strangelove, and although the VTC was supposed to be a three-line whip, I seldom attended after that, too depressing.

Meanwhile matters became increasingly heated in Thessaloniki, and NATO began to wonder how long it could maintain the HQ there which serviced ARRC's maritime route in and out of the operational theatre. There was an alternative, albeit requiring an extremely roundabout route through Bulgaria, which fortunately had been a PfP nation since 1994.

My office was asked to look into any legal feasibility issues with such a contingency, rather a 'fast ball' but we were starting to get used to them. The possible sticking point turned out to be the 1936 Montreux Convention, the most recent of a number of treaties governing the rights of passage of shipping through the Dardanelles and Bosphorus Straits between the Black Sea and the Mediterranean. These are Turkish waters, and it turned out that the convention essentially grants Turkey the discretion to regulate the passage of shipping, in particular warships. Turkey being a NATO member, it looked as if this might be an option if necessary.

Next up was, of all things, an intervention under the 1994 Vienna CSBM Agreement[22] which enabled countries to demand full details of the disposition of military formations in Europe (such as ours) outside their peacetime locations. Yugoslavia was not a party to this but their ally Belorussia, which was, kindly obliged them by making a formal declaration under the agreement, requesting an inspection. Our CDS, General Guthrie, was visiting Skopje at the time and was highly unamused at what he clearly regarded as a despicable ploy, stating point blank that it was not to happen. My new Brit SO2, Richard Batty, who had then also just arrived at Main, made himself thoroughly unpopular by pointing out that he didn't think NATO had any option, which proved correct.

Richard was on the spot because we swapped locations during some of May, so it was he and Bart who ended up dealing with the inspection, a lot of work, which they handled brilliantly. I spent a little time minding the shop back at JHQ where a spell of home comfort was very welcome.

After the uncertainties of life in the shoe factory, the atmosphere at Rheindahlen was rather surreal, with wonderful spring weather, the neatness of the German countryside in sharp contrast to poor scruffy old Skopje. However, even back home some evenings vividly reminded us of what was going on a few hundred miles away as the Tornados from RAF Bruggen took off over our heads with a shattering roar, afterburners glowing as they set off to the southeast on their bombing sorties. Having been established as an RAF base since the end of the Second World War, this was the first and last offensive operation ever to be launched from Bruggen, which closed a few years later.

By the time I returned to Skopje, the air campaign which was supposed to have lasted just a few days had been going on for nearly seventy and as NATO literally started to run out of targets and bombs, tension on all sides was running high. There had been some serious mistakes, like the unintended bombing of the Thessaloniki–Belgrade express train as it ran into the path of an attack intended for the bridge it was crossing. This inevitably strained NATO's resolve to the limit as the already angry Greek general public suffered a number of victims. One night in early May another US attack had hit the Chinese embassy in Belgrade, apparently because the wrong maps had been used, so incredible it might almost have been true, and another night the Belgrade radio station was also destroyed, arguably a lawful military objective, but very controversial.[23]

The Yugoslavs were defiant, but inexorably becoming war weary, as the targets increasingly expanded beyond Kosovo itself[24] and the associated economic hardships also began to bite, while NATO had yet to sustain a single fatality. Russia, whose weight was theoretically firmly behind Milosevic, finally acknowledged that he could not survive much longer and despite uttering blood-curdling threats of the consequences if NATO did not desist, made it clear to him that he was on his own.

But when the beginning of the end did come it was almost out of the blue. No sooner had I arrived back at the shoe factory[25] than word reached us by video conference in the ARRC that General Jackson was to meet a Yugoslav Army delegation on the FYROM/Kosovo border for talks[26] the following morning.

The first day's 'talks' were inconclusive and neither party found the Europa roadside café a very convenient location. From our point of view, it was important to have access to properly organized, secure communications and decent accommodation and catering facilities for a process which was clearly going to take a while. For the Yugoslavs, the requirement to drive backwards and forwards from Belgrade through the heart of Kosovo was more than just uncomfortable; this was a very senior military delegation which would have been an extremely juicy target for a random UCK roadblock in the province to get their hands on.

The solution was to move to the Kumanovo military airbase, currently occupied by French KFOR troops, which had all the logistic advantages which we needed and was adjacent to the Serbian border next to Kosovo, not Kosovo itself, thereby avoiding the other party running that dangerous gauntlet.

I joined General Jackson and his entourage toing and froing the short distance from Skopje by Lynx helicopter, as part of what can best be described as a travelling circus which lasted a couple of days before matters were finally resolved.[27] A huge inflatable marquee resembling a bouncy castle was kitted out for the talks, with enough seating for the UN General Assembly, only for a decision then to be made that all that was really needed was a 12x12 army tent. The talks went on late into the nights, in an atmosphere of high drama, with no more than a handful of participants,[28] seated on canvas chairs around trestle tables in the brightly lit tent itself – it could have been Luneburg Heath in 1945 – staked out by 'close protection' hoods, and a hushed audience of us lesser KFOR mortals on hand at a discreet distance, just out of earshot.

The eyes of the world were on this balmy backwater and the media descended en masse, with TV cameras swivelling backwards and forwards like spectators' heads at Wimbledon, but they appeared to have trouble adjusting to the fact that the talks could occupy such a modest venue and persisted in focusing on the bouncy castle instead. We decided not to let on, as their confusion actually suited the parties, enabling them to get on with the business at hand in peace and quiet.

The French had taken to the task of hosting this significant milestone in the operation with a combination of military efficiency and Gallic gastronomical *élan*. This was not lost on the Yugoslavs, who, when summoned back to Belgrade in the evening for further instructions, crammed the boots of their little convoy of battered Mercedes with every last one of the cans of Pelforth and Orangina, vol au vents, petits saucissons, baguettes and patisseries left over from the day's catering. 'They've looted the place!' said General Ridgway.

The Yugoslavs returned the following day but by mid-afternoon they appeared to have had enough and jumped into their cars to head north once again, pausing only to refill their boots with refreshments. The cameras followed the somewhat dejected KFOR delegation back to the Lynxes as we prepared to return to Skopje after yet another fruitless day. We were literally about to board the aircraft when we received word that the Yugoslavs had turned round and were on their way back, having been ordered by Belgrade to 'put a swift end to this matter'. So, the Wimbledon swivel followed us all back off the aircraft, accompanied by frantic speculation as to what the hell was going on now.

I must say it did occur to me that the Yugoslavs' words could mean one of two things and maybe it was all off, and indeed, as the hours ticked by, the outcome looked increasingly doubtful, but finally wisps of white smoke were metaphorically seen wafting from the tent and the deed was done.

The atmosphere was electric, with the press jostling for pole position to hear what Jacko had to announce to the world, but this excitement began to turn to exasperation and impatience as the minutes passed. The cameramen amused themselves filming a Lynx taking off for the south and again as it returned about half an hour later but could throw no more light on the cause of yet another delay in this tortuous process.

Meanwhile, the respective delegations in the tent tucked into some celebratory French *amuses-bouches* and finally, shortly after a Lynx crewman had delivered a small parcel, they emerged. The Yugoslavs headed home again, but this time General Jackson was striding to the press podium, with a weary but relieved smile on his face, to announce that an agreement had finally been signed.

If only Slobodan himself had been there, he would have observed that the reason the most powerful military/political alliance in history had had to call 'time out' at the eleventh hour was that they had run out of paper. For reasons of time-honoured protocol, the agreement which had been struck had to be signed on exactly the right stationery, which was in limited supply, and so many drafts had been scrapped that when it came to the final version there was none left. Hence that last Lynx shuttle to Skopje and back, and the mysterious parcel delivery.

The Military Technical Agreement (MTA) which had been the cause of such prolonged agonizing was just one of a number of pieces in a diplomatic jigsaw which had to be assembled in order to bring this conflict to a practical and secure conclusion. As its name suggests, the purpose of this first piece was to enable a smooth transition from the occupation of Kosovo by Yugoslav national forces to an immediate replacement by UN-sanctioned KFOR forces.

Perhaps the most important provision of the arrangements was to guarantee as far as humanly possible that there would be no 'security vacuum' allowed to develop within the territory between departing Yugoslavs and KFOR on their heels, as it was clear that any such vacuum could and undoubtedly would be exploited by the UCK, with deadly consequences for anybody who got in their way.

Preventing the risk of this eventuality called for some extremely delicate logistical planning, especially as the five different KFOR national formations would be entering Kosovo by different routes, none of which was likely to be particularly secure, or indeed necessarily intact thanks to the work of their comrades in the air over the preceding weeks. Their timing and coordination, both with each other on their flanks and the Yugoslavs ahead of them, as they moved to take up their assigned areas of responsibility within Kosovo had to be spot on.

That was not the only critical chronological element of this whole process; each piece of the diplomatic jigsaw also had to be put in place in precisely the right order. By 9 June, the date the MTA was signed, the UN had secured the agreement of the Security Council to the terms of a draft resolution to enshrine the KFOR/Serb agreement for the short- to mid-term status of Kosovo in international law. The resolution could not be passed while the air campaign continued[29] but NATO would not suspend the bombing without the MTA being signed and a 'verifiable' withdrawal of some of the Serb forces from Kosovo, knowing that once suspended there would be no prospect of resuming it[30] should the Serbs renege.

However, after the signing on the 9th, the air campaign was duly suspended and, on the 10th, UNSCR 1244 was passed (a matter of some relief, because it could still have been vetoed even then). This still left additional pieces of the jigsaw to be added in order to complete it, as the UCK were not parties to any agreement yet but that could only follow in days to come.

Meanwhile the wily fox Milosevic, far from conceding that he had finally been defeated by these developments, hailed the fortitude of his people in holding out against the aggressive might of NATO, exacting the very concessions at the negotiating table which the West had refused him at Rambouillet.

To be honest, he had a point. The reader will recall that the 'take it or leave it' Rambouillet terms which Serbia declined included a demand that the force occupying Kosovo should have unlimited freedom of movement throughout, not just that province, but the whole of Serbia. The MTA signed at Kumanovo limits KFOR to Kosovo only. Secondly, and equally significant, at Rambouillet Kosovo's status as part of Yugoslavia was up for grabs but under UNSCR 1244 it is specifically referred to as a part of Yugoslav sovereign territory.

The MTA was almost silent on one important aspect of KFOR's activities once they finally entered Kosovo, namely its operational legal status. The law of 'occupation', a mixture of customary international law, nineteenth-century Hague regulations and the 4th Geneva Convention of 1949 contains very specific provisions for occupying forces during 'belligerent occupation'. However, as this occupation would be by agreement as opposed to invasion, those provisions did not apply.[31] The conventional arrangement for regulating relations between host nation (Serbia in this case) and visiting forces (KFOR) is the familiar SOFA and in fact my limited input to the discussions had largely been a conversation with General Jackson when he asked, 'Jim, the Serbs are asking about a SOFA – there should be one, shouldn't there?'

To which the answer was certainly there should. The problem was that the talks had been so hurried that nobody had devised a SOFA for inclusion. The solution adopted was to include within the MTA a commitment by both parties to negotiate a SOFA as soon as possible. Thereby hangs a tale, as we shall see.

Back at the shoe factory, COMARRC modestly acknowledged a flood of thoroughly deserved congratulations from all directions on his determined and sensitive handling of recent events, but just as the real ones stopped falling, a metaphorical bombshell silenced our euphoria.

Yet again it was at a VTC[32] that we first heard a rumour, which was rapidly confirmed, that a Russian formation at SFOR[33] was preparing to drive from there through Serbia to secure Pristina airport before KFOR arrived, having replaced the "S" in SFOR on their vehicles with a K (and allegedly promoted the one-star formation commander to four star in order to outrank Jacko!). SACEUR, whose short fuse was by

The Front-line Factory

now familiar, was almost literally ballistic, ordering COMSFOR, a US general in his NATO chain of command, to stop the Russians moving. This was met with something of a Nelson touch, and sure enough the Russians were coming.

Much has been made of the ensuing row between Jacko and Wes Clark, who ordered him to use any means necessary to prevent the Russians securing the airport.[34] From my own experience on the scene I know that whether or not he actually used the words 'I am not going to start World War Three for you', COMARRC was clearly determined not to allow this development to derail the MTA, but instead to treat the Russians as potential allies, with whom we would cooperate, and from whom in turn we would seek realistic cooperation. As history records, thankfully he was able to pull this off, equipped as he was with the perfect combination of a command of Russian language and a flask of Scotch.[35] both of which he skilfully deployed during a rain-soaked meeting at Pristina airport, having taken the risk of flying up there to meet the Russian commander.

Before that happy outcome was achieved, however, all sorts of very alarming contingencies had to be contemplated. This was such an unexpected intervention that nobody at strategic level back in Belgium had even considered it, and my position in the food chain jumped to the point that I was summoned to a Corps planning group meeting in which I was asked for legal advice on 'Rules of Engagement with the Russians'. My response was that I did not believe we would be engaging the Russians with armed force and I hoped very much we were going to be grown up about this. For me, that short meeting ranked alongside the night time 'artillery barrage that never was' a few weeks earlier, as the most frightening moment of the operation.

What motivated the Russians? They had played a crucial role; indeed, some would say *the* crucial role in bringing matters thus far by diplomatic means, yet here they were about to be completely side-lined by NATO on their front doorstep. Maybe there was also something nasty or just precious to the Russians hidden on or below Pristina airbase which they wanted to extract before NATO got there, who knows?

One serious theory was that Milosevic had done a deal with Russia whereby they would combine with those Serb forces still present in northern Kosovo and just sit there, defying NATO to enforce the MTA militarily to evict them from a de facto partitioned province. Russia, knowing its small SFOR unit was unsustainable on its own, certainly tried to reinforce by air, only to be denied overflight from Russian soil by some intervening countries which a few years earlier would not have dared to refuse.

Finally, everybody calmed down. With a huge collective sigh of relief, we were able to revert to the original plan, and Operation Joint Guardian finally kicked off, with the first KFOR troops entering Kosovo via the notorious 'Kacanik defile' through the hills at 5 am on 12 June, the date picked by Richard Batty in the HQ sweepstake. Jacko personally presented him his prize, with Richard rather cheekily congratulating the general on his 'immaculate timing'. Bart missed all this excitement, as it was his turn to take some leave, to be at the birth of his son back in the Netherlands.

On the 15th, leaving Richard to man the desk in Skopje, I deployed to Kosovo with the commander's tactical HQ. We flew up from Kumanovo at dusk in a heavily laden Chinook through the mountains along the border, a flight which was apparently as much of a journey into the unknown for the pilot as the rest of us. We seemed to be ducking and diving, with hillsides appearing every now and then out of heavy clouds, alarmingly close, through the portholes. We were lost, and at one point my neighbour shouted in my ear 'We're turning back,' but eventually, guided down by what appeared to be a single torch, we touched down in a field just outside Pristina.

Chapter 4

The Lord Chief Justice of Kosovo

This clandestine arrival of our Tac HQ contrasted sharply with the triumphant entry of the bulk of KFOR soldiers into Kosovo as broadcast by the world's media, with crowds of delighted locals showering the boys with flowers and kisses, like General Mark Clark's army entering Rome in June 1944, amid ecstatic chants of 'NATO, NATO'. Sadly, in our little HQ we were deprived of all this euphoria as there was still much staff work to be done.

Our initial home in Pristina made the shoe factory look like the Ritz. We slept in tents pitched on the rubble floor of a derelict warehouse next to a stagnant, evil-smelling pond in the middle of a field, gently illuminated on the night of our arrival by a merrily burning house a short distance away. Here we were to stay for several days and nights, working out of the back of trucks, entertained by the sounds of Serb T-55 tanks rolling north by day and small-arms fire by night. For a while it was just nice to be out in the open for a change but then a monsoon descended, turning the terrain into Passchendaele and making life generally pretty miserable.

At dead of night, on 20 June, we were joined in our quagmire by numerous new characters in the cast of our ongoing drama, fresh from Albania. These included Lieutenant-General John Reith, commander AFOR,[1] General Agim Ceku[2] of the UCK, who would be our principal interlocutor in dealings with them in the following weeks, and Hashim Thaci, their C-in-C. This slightly sinister assembly was bolstered from the West by other equally interesting characters from the world of spin, such as James Rubin, US State Department, and Alistair Campbell, Downing Street.

The purpose of this somewhat shady gathering was for the KLA/UCK to present COMKFOR their 'Undertaking of Demilitarization and Transformation', the next piece of the diplomatic jigsaw, to sit beside the MTA. The substance of the undertaking was principally a complex timetable for the cantonment of UCK personnel, decommissioning of weapons, abandonment of military insignia and a variety of other quasi-legal provisions which entailed lengthy deliberation and horse-trading in the weeks to come.

Greater legal minds than mine insisted General Jackson should only acknowledge the document by indicating that he had 'received' it, not that he 'accepted' it, although if I ever understood the reasoning behind these linguistic gymnastics, it escapes me now. On the night, however, we spent some considerable time trying to discover the appropriate words in the Albanian language to make the necessary distinction.

Through the interpreter, I suggested the formula of a dinner party invitation, distinguishing between 'receiving' the stiffy through the letterbox and subsequently indicating that I would be delighted to attend, that is, 'accepting' the invitation. However, it soon became evident that Thaci was not a regular dinner party guest, as the different concepts were completely lost on him and we eventually concluded that there was only one word in Albanian to convey both meanings. So, after this supposedly crucial issue had consumed several hours of high-level tooth-sucking it was quietly dropped, and at ten past midnight on the morning of the summer solstice Thaci signed and COMKFOR received/accepted.

The next day I went with a number of colleagues for a recce of the establishment which had been identified as our permanent Pristina HQ, a former film studio complex on a hill overlooking the city, known as 'Film City', but which we soon re christened 'Planet Hollywood'. If I was scathing about the architecture in Skopje, it was nothing compared to this monstrosity, with a cavernous, half-completed 'bat cave' for a conference room in the bowels of the building, and external rendering in a tasteful bilious yellow.

Having said that, if you accept the estate agent's mantra of 'Location, location, location', it was fine for us, a secure spot, with a commanding view and plenty of space for parking, helicopters, and tented accommodation outside. In fact, by the time we moved in a few days later the weather had cleared up and, having spent the last few months cooped up first in a factory and then in our muddy warehouse, taking up residence in a tent in the woods at the back of the building (complete with dubious sanitation) felt very like starting a camping holiday.

Pristina itself had not been anything like as severely trashed as CNN, Jamie Shea or the USAF had had us believe. It clearly had never been blessed with the civic pride of Vienna but most of it was more or less intact. Exceptions were the MUP HQ building, the VJ barracks, and a large fuel storage depot, all of which were in a bad way, the latter with a car rather spectacularly launched upside down onto the roof of a neighbouring building.

The destruction hadn't finished, however, as most evenings we could look out from the Film City balcony over house fires raging in the Serb and Roma quarters of town. Such voyeurism was soon discouraged after a couple of occasions when we appeared to be the targets ourselves of random potshots and on one particularly wild Friday night Lieutenant-Colonel Paul Gibson,[3] CO of the Para battalion on security duties downtown described it as 'like bloody *Bladerunner* down here'.

Slowly but surely the various elements of KFOR settled into their respective areas of operation, trying their best to keep a lid on an excitable and largely lawless population until such time as some sort of conventional administration took over. The strategy involved the establishment of a UN mission, UNMIK, but that could not begin to happen at least until life became reasonably secure. Partly to that end KFOR HQ rapidly established a 'Joint Implementation Commission' to thrash out with the KLA the realization of the timetables in their undertaking. The main aims were demobilization and disarmament, to convert them from fighters in a triumphant but volatile rebel army to responsible, impartial civilians playing their part in establishing a stable and, above all, peaceful future for the province.[4]

The most positive initial consequence of the events of that June was the rapid return of tens of thousands of refugees from their makeshift camps in FYROM and Albania, a powerful vindication of the whole operation so far. However, although problems with the security situation were entirely predictable, the fact that neither Rambouillet nor the air campaign had gone to plan meant that both the UN and NATO were ill prepared when the dam burst and we suddenly found ourselves on the ground at our destination.

It had never been anticipated that Kosovo would be left entirely devoid of key personnel to run the place when NATO arrived but that is just exactly what we found. The bitterness between Serbs and Albanian Kosovars had inevitably only become exacerbated by the bombing so that the terms of the MTA required all Serb government forces to withdraw. This meant, of course, that there were no police left in the province whatsoever when we arrived.

A perfect storm erupted, as the civilian Serb population was understandably terrified that they would be subjected to bloody revenge by the ethnic Albanian majority without even their own police there to protect them, so most of them fled. This in turn meant that all the other infrastructure, from power stations to hospitals was suddenly emasculated, as all senior professional and management positions had been held by Serbs.

One of the most serious consequences of that was that the criminal justice system collapsed, not only devoid of police but also prosecutors and judges, just at a time when the Albanians, returning in their thousands from exile, saw carte blanche to embark on an unprecedented crime wave. The opportunities not only for revenge against their Serb neighbours but for good old-fashioned looting and pillaging of hurriedly deserted properties were too good to be true.

Those first few weeks in Kosovo were a tremendous challenge for KFOR[5] at all levels, not least in the HQ legal branch, and in the absence of any legal authorities for the foreseeable future, Jacko dubbed me the 'Lord Chief Justice of Kosovo'. Of course, this was very much tongue in cheek but it was in a way a proud moment and certainly not one I could ever have anticipated whilst slaving away before the 'dictators' of Guildford.

It was no sinecure, and I hardly knew where to begin with the legal problems which the situation presented. First, what about jurisdiction?

We were on sovereign Serb territory, even UNSCR 1244 confirmed that, so under the principle of territorial jurisdiction Serb law must apply, including the criminal law relating to what was and was not an offence, arrest, detention, bail, remand, charging, custody, prosecution, rules of evidence and procedure, sentencing etc. etc. In anticipation of this I had made some attempt at studying translated Serb criminal law texts while back in Skopje, but my knowledge was pretty limited. I also had to consider the extent to which the UNSCR mandate empowered COMKFOR to issue decrees under its 'all necessary measures' catch-all provision.

Shortly after arrival in Pristina I was very grateful to receive reinforcements in the shape of Jo Bowen, a keen volunteer for life at the sharp end who was lent to me by the UK Logistics Brigade and soon Bart also returned from his paternal duties. However, the other people on the ground responsible for dealing with the law and order task came from five different nations, all with their own domestic versions of the relevant legal provisions. They were also all bound by customary human rights law, and four out of five of them by the European Convention on Human Rights.

The fifth, the USA, was obviously not an ECHR state party and also had a tendency to apply the notion of 'exceptionalism' to a lot of what it did, including the application of military authority. So, at least initially, we had five different ways of policing this law and order nightmare in five different assigned areas of operations, and somehow we at the HQ had to try and devise a fair, lawful and consistent practice across all five, starting pretty much from scratch.

It was much easier in some cases than others. The French and Italians were philosophically pretty liberal, and COMKFOR became very exercised at times when hearing of looters detained one day, only to be found the next day in the same town committing the same offences, because the forces would refuse to hold them for more than a few hours before releasing them back on to the streets.

The French have their Gendarmerie and the Italians the Carabinieri, so once some of them deployed into province those nations were better able to cope (irrespective of jokes about pasta, *passeggiata* and the priority of wearing a cool uniform). On the other side of the coin, neither the French nor the Italians initially had military legal officers on their strength, making my liaison with them that much more problematic. The Brits, the Germans and the Americans were a little more robust from the outset, although the latter were severely handicapped by occupying an entirely tented HQ,[6] with no secure building available for the incarceration of serious criminals.[7]

Unlike in FYROM, we did at least have the benefit of a set of ROE issued by NATO for Kosovo, including ROE cards, an essential in every soldier's back pocket to keep him on the straight and narrow, although even getting them signed off by our higher HQ before we went in was a cliff-hanger. Historically, soldiers have had little to do with arresting and detaining good ordinary criminals, as opposed to prisoners of war, but that is no longer the case. As one-time UN Secretary-General Dag Hammerskjöld said: 'Peacekeeping is not a job for soldiers but only soldiers can do it.'

We immediately had a problem with the Kosovo ROE because NATO had prepared them months ago on the assumption of a Rambouillet-type settlement which would see Yugoslav police still operating in Kosovo, with

KFOR merely alongside them. Consequently, there were serious holes in what the rules permitted. Thus I became involved in another rather bad-tempered email exchange with AFSouth; this is just one example:

Me: 'It's no good having rules which only permit KFOR to arrest for offences committed *"in the presence of members of NATO forces"* because we are the only people in town to arrest anyone for anything and we need to be able to deal with offences even if we didn't witness them – please forward the following ROE request for amendment …'

The reply: 'COMKFOR has authority under the UNSCR to use "all necessary measures" to carry out his mission, so that can include any arrest and detention and there's no need for the ROE to be amended.'

And mine: 'OK, in that case why do we bother with ROE at all?'

No answer – and there never was – all too difficult for those in the rear. It wasn't me who would suffer, but the prisoner who was mistreated, or the soldier who was later charged with some offence for technically breaching his ROE, or even the nation in the dock at the European Court of Human Rights in Strasbourg who would pay the price. However, events were moving too fast to spend too much time just on that battle, so we noted it for now and moved on.

When the issue of arrest had been licked into some sort of consistent shape, we had to work out what to do with the prisoners longer term, and embarked on a province-wide hunt for legally qualified prosecutors and judges, courtrooms, prisons and warders. Having eventually achieved that too, we had to beg, steal and borrow helicopters to get the lawyers safely to and from court, then having to cajole them to board the unfamiliar aircraft, of which most of them were terrified.

The other fundamental legal matter which required my urgent attention was the SOFA. Much of KFOR's business on entering Kosovo involved enforcing compliance by the Serbs with the MTA, and by the UCK with their undertaking. Our credibility in achieving this was dependent on our own compliance, part of which required us to negotiate a SOFA without delay.

AFSouth were completely out of the loop and apparently unsighted on the issue, so when I first raised the problem with them, they said they didn't know how the SOFA commitment 'got into' the MTA. As I pointed out, this was neither here nor there; it was in there and it needed to be addressed. I was told it would be 'political madness' to start engaging with the Serbs on such matters, to which my response was, among other things, that I thought we were engaged in giving legal advice, not politics.

There followed lengthy emails between AFSOUTH and SHAPE which only confirmed disarray above our heads as to NATO's approach to the serious legal issues we were facing on the ground. I rapidly became hugely frustrated with the lack of coherent, constructive input, as evidenced by an email I sent to the KFOR liaison officer in Naples on 20 June, which went something like this:

> I am afraid the tennis match between AFSOUTH and SHAPE as to how we might deal with these issues is not helping us one bit.
>
> First, on the subject of SOFAs, the senior NATO lawyer, Mr De Vidts has been tasked to seek NATO's comments on the original Rambouillet SOFA with a view to a slightly tweaked version being presented to the NAC, and thence to Belgrade for signature but I am advised by AFSOUTH that no such thing must happen. So, which is the true situation?
>
> Indeed, we have also been asked to comment, so are we wasting our time or not, please?! Certainly, if the UN are negotiating a SOMA[8] with Belgrade it would seem utterly illogical if we refuse to negotiate a SOFA, particularly as we undertook to do so in the MTA. We will be non-compliant and probably accused of lacking good faith if we decline to do so.
>
> I seem to have seen in UNSCR 1244 a declaration acknowledging the territorial integrity of the FRY, which includes Kosovo, irrespective of the interim administration of UNMIK. Can somebody please quote me as a simple lawyer the legal authority as opposed to the political spin for declining to negotiate a SOFA with the sovereign Government of the FRY as soon as possible. I understand that the decision about this simple SOFA issue will be made way above my pay grade, but it is extremely difficult for me to advise my commander of the situation when I get a fax from Mr De Vidts inviting my comments on the Rambouillet SOFA and then messages from AFSOUTH that no such SOFA is intended!

As for ROE, we have already explained in detail what we feel we need, but we are just having to manage as we are, impotent to do otherwise in the absence of any action from above.

As for detainees, and law and order generally, I have a real question for guidance upon, not hypothetical. Our mandate to maintain law and order has begun, and already we are detaining approx 16 people for serious offences, including murder. What does AFSOUTH suggest we do with them? It is all very well saying the UN will take on the law and order issue, but the issue is already here, so are we, but the UN is not, except in very small representative numbers.

Obviously, we cannot turn people like this loose, but may we please have some higher authority advice on our detention provisions, whereby we avoid any risk of falling foul of the national jurisdiction of the detaining nations, which include the US and/or the ECHR.

This issue is bound to increase considerably as time goes by. We have only been here a week and we already have the number stated, and this is before most of the refugee population of approx 900,000 have returned, as they are now beginning to do. We know better than anybody else what the problems are, we don't need reminding of them, or having additional ones hypothesized, we need guidance.

We are handling the detainees according to the best regime we can devise, but we have no policy advice from above, except 'it would be quite wrong to put KFOR in the position of overseeing human rights'. With respect, Colonel, we are already in that position, whether we like it or not. Who else do you suggest at this time, there is nobody else here but us? We cannot trust the domestic judicial system, and it will be weeks before any civilian agency such as the OSCE[9] will be here in anything like the necessary numbers to begin to fulfil the tasks of police and judiciary.

We look forward to detailed *guidance* as soon as possible.

Needless to say, my hopes for a detailed response were unfulfilled, but I later had a couple of refreshing days back in Belgium to attend a meeting at SHAPE at which the senior NATO legal staff listened politely to AFSouth but concluded that the recommendation to Javier Solana, NATO Secretary-General, would be that a SOFA was necessary. It wasn't rocket science; for example, the UN had a template which could easily be adapted. I returned to Pristina quite pleased with having a few days away, but also to be able to tell the boss that all was well and a SOFA would be provided by SHAPE in the near future.

However, just a few days later I received an exasperated message from Nigel Jones at SHAPE:

> You may know that the US have stated their firm objection to negotiating a SOFA with the FRY. I spoke to ... PJHQ[10] today who confirmed that the UK has decided to follow the US view, despite legal advice to the contrary. So, it seems that for the short term we will not get what we want/need. No change there then.

There was no further explanation, but clearly somebody in Washington had decided to trump NATO. I duly informed Jacko, strongly suspecting from his polite but relaxed response that he had already been told.

It was not such a big deal in practice; if we imported stuff we shouldn't import, who was going to charge a tariff? If a soldier broke Serbian law, who was going to arrest him? But I found this approach extremely frustrating and it offended my sense of propriety and the integrity of what we were supposed to represent. Along with all the ROE problems, it added a nail in the coffin of my faith in 'the system'; there was only one 'mighty' party in play and still apparently 'might is right', which was not how I understood the rule of law.

The combination of COMKFOR's experience and level head, with first-class staff both in his own office[11] and in the various KFOR brigade HQs, and unexpectedly good cooperation from both Serb and KLA protagonists, made for steady progress on the ground despite the absence of guidance from above us in the chain of command.

The MTA timetable was adhered to, the KLA (mostly) disarmed on time and the Serbs, despite intermittent grumbling propaganda from Belgrade, complied with the UN. We just had to 'fudge' the issues of the deficient ROE and absent SOFA, with COMKFOR effectively ruling by a combination of decree and what the US call 'law by analogy', or pragmatic policy directions on issues such as arrest and detention, until such time as UNMIK were able to take over.

Once we had the legal office properly up and running, we established a very useful network of legal advisors throughout the different KFOR formations, an essential for achieving the consistency in criminal justice which was required, holding a 'summit' for them later in June which then became a valuable monthly event. We were also careful to ensure we kept the ICRC and leading NGOs informed of what we were doing, and why, securing their endorsement of our methodology which relieved us of a potentially major headache down the track. Bitter experience in subsequent operations has shown that failure to secure such endorsement can expose soldiers and commanders alike to an avalanche of often financially or politically motivated law suits, nowadays dubbed 'Lawfare'.[12] Our early day efforts in Kosovo were fraught with such legal risks but even after the dust had settled and hindsight kicked in, KFOR remained litigation free.

I decided it was time to get out and about a bit, to have a look at this unfamiliar country which had dominated my working life for the past eighteen months. It was also important to visit my opposite numbers at each national HQ to find out how they were coping with their legal problems, to fly the HQ KFOR flag and to try and ensure they understood and implemented the commander's intent regarding law and order issues, so Jo and I took a road trip.

The countryside in the summer was gentle and beautiful, poor but 'bucolic', in stark contrast with the sinister landscape of the northern Balkans in winter. The agricultural technology seemed in many ways pre-industrial revolution, with the corn (mostly milled to make the most wonderful bread), reaped by scythe and carted behind horses, and the straw later stored in conical stooks in the open, like a scene from Thomas Hardy's *Far from the Madding Crowd*. Modernity did exist, in the form of the ubiquitous little red tractors, towing small trailers containing large Albanian families on their way to and from market. The status symbol du jour was a middle-aged Mercedes, freshly stolen and still brazenly bearing its D sticker and German number plates.

Out in the sticks, signs of the bombing were remarkably few and far between, and even there my impression that we had heard a lot of hype was confirmed by what I saw. Like Pristina, the towns were all pretty run down but this was clearly far more the effect of years of economic stagnation than recent attention from the air. The main exception was on the roads, where we had to make several detours where bridges had been taken out, although on one occasion we copied the locals and took a chance with our Land Rover, crossing one which although technically still standing was very wobbly. We also saw some examples of the Serbs' camouflaging ingenuity, with fake bridges erected close to real ones which had been concealed, and green painted sheds with drainpipes sticking out of them, to look like tanks from the air.

Such was the level of political interest in how many targets had actually been hit that we hosted a team at the film factory for a couple of weeks led by a USAF colonel, called the Mission Effectiveness Assessment Team (MEAT), sent down from SHAPE to investigate. They spent their time flitting around the province by helicopter, trying to identify targets which had been damaged or destroyed. On more than one occasion they identified such targets, only to find on swooping lower for confirmation that it was in fact one of the little green sheds. If you can make that mistake from an aircraft flying at 1,500 feet and 80 knots it is little surprise that mistakes were made by F-16s at 20,000 feet and 300 knots. The MEAT's findings were 'disappointing', and further inquiry was discouraged.

A number of mass graves were found dotted around the province[13] which added to the tension on the ground and KFOR were sadly unable to prevent a number of revenge killings. I declined an invitation for a ghoulish visit to one of these sites but I was shown a blood-spattered torture chamber, complete with electrodes, within the main police station in Pec, now occupied by Italian troops. Later, in Mitrovica, which was now French-occupied I was shown around the central prison in which they were holding remand prisoners – an edifice straight out of *Midnight Express*.

It wasn't just in Kosovo that legal issues remained unresolved, however; tensions with the Greeks were still causing problems way back at Thessaloniki. There was no lawyer there to reassure the rear support commander, and having been reinforced still further up in Pristina, I felt I could afford the luxury of a quick visit to Greece to see for myself.

Although it seemed a world away, Thessaloniki was only about 350 kilometres away by road and Bart and I drove down in a day. I knew some of the route as far as Skopje, now largely devoid of the refugee camps which had lined it when I was last there, but FYROM south of the capital was new to me. The traffic was light and the road was unexpectedly well maintained, passing through mile after mile of sun-drenched vineyards, but as we entered Greece the atmosphere changed tangibly, with every bridge daubed with strident anti-NATO graffiti. Nevertheless, despite some residual nervousness following previous attacks on the camp, morale at RSC seemed high and although the whole issue of legal status there was, surprise surprise, also unresolved, due this time to Greek bureaucratic inertia, the colonel in command seemed quite relaxed about it all.

We stayed one night and on setting off back the next morning we were surprised to notice a substantial naval presence in Thessaloniki Bay. This turned out to be the US 26th Marine Expeditionary Unit (26 MEU) awaiting disembarkation, to come and augment the US 1st Infantry Division at Camp Bond Steel up in Kosovo. Apparently, it is against the US Marines' religion to disembark the easy way, via a harbour facility like anyone else, and they have to come up the beach even when unopposed. We missed that spectacle, but we were treated to an equally unexpected one a few kilometres up the road.

As we rounded a long sweeping stretch of dual carriageway just back inside FYROM, we had to slow down rapidly for the tail of a military convoy stretching for several kilometres ahead of us. This, by way of contrast, turned out to be the Russians. After the little awkwardness at Pristina airport a few weeks ago, we were all friends now and it had been arranged that a substantial Russian unit would join KFOR.

The convoy we were now overtaking was trundling along at a steady 50 kph, which seemed unnecessarily slow until on closer inspection it appeared that the vehicles were so old and knackered that they could have come straight from Stalingrad. This was many years before Putin had got a grip and modernized the Russian armed forces and the snail's pace was dictated by a combination of frequent breakdowns and the need for fuel economy.

A few days after my return to Pristina I received a message from AFSouth which was, for once, helpful and welcome: an offer of further reinforcement. It seemed that the US MEU had now scrambled up the beach in Greece and arrived in Kosovo with a surplus of legal (US JAG Corps) officers, and would I like to borrow a major? I was slightly suspicious that this was some sort of Trojan horse and I was to be spied upon, because I had no doubt AFSouth regarded me as thoroughly awkward following our numerous spats but it would have been ungracious to refuse, and an extra body would always be useful.

Hence, we welcomed Major Brian Palmer of the USMC a few days later. Shortly after he arrived, brushing the Greek sand off his boots, I couldn't resist probing the reasons for him joining us: 'Brian, we're quite a long way from the sea here and as a Marine you must feel a bit lost, don't you?'

'Oh no – I hate the sea.'

'You hate the sea! You could have joined the army or the air force as a JAG officer and never gone near the sea, so why on earth would you join the Marine Corps?'

'That's easy: it was because the army and air force don't require much military training for their JAG officers but when you join the Marines you have to do the whole *Full Metal Jacket* thing.'

So, although he didn't look it, it appeared that Brian was one of those slightly masochistic types you often come across in the services, especially US, who actually enjoy that sort of hair-shirted stuff. However, whether or not he had actually been sent to keep an eye on us, he turned out to be not only a thoroughly nice colleague to have around but a very sound operator. Brian had never served outside any US national unit before so there was a lot to learn and he clearly relished the novelty of being in a British-run multinational HQ, declaring almost immediately the superiority of Land Rovers over Humvees.

Our 'cookhouse', a pair of large marquees out in the woods next to the dormitory tents, was run by the Brits and the food was second to none. I decided that our cuisine was a fundamental essential for Brian's education. We struck gold at lunchtime on his first day with us, as among other items on the menu board was 'Faggots in onion gravy'.

'Brian,' I said, 'that's what you have to choose today – food doesn't get much more British than faggots.'

'Faggots!' he blurted out with a look of mixed alarm and bewilderment. 'How could I tell my wife I had faggots?'[14]

The next day I tried again: 'OK, today you must have the steak and kidney pie,'

'You mean real kidney?'

'Of course.'

'I never ate an organ in my life.'

He took it all in good humour and although sadly Bart had departed back to Skopje by now, we had a very happy office, with Richard Batty arriving in his place.

Brian was very soon put to work on a US-specific legal question of strategic importance. The US have a very strict 'General Order No. 1' which absolutely forbids the consumption of alcohol by US servicemen deployed on operations. We had a very popular beer tent in the woods but General Maples, our US one-star, assumed GO#1 applied, so he never indulged, and all other US staff dutifully followed his example. However, at about the time of Brian's arrival, General Maples moved on and his successor, Brigadier-General William Brandenburg, who was evidently a social animal, queried whether the order strictly applied to US servicemen in a multinational, as opposed to a US national, HQ. Spotting our tame JAG officer, he asked for a legal opinion on the matter. Just from the fact that he'd asked the question it was very obvious what answer he was hoping for.

Brian was concerned to get this right, and asked me, 'What do you think, Colonel Jim? I'm sure Wes Clark would want the rule to apply even here.'

'You're probably right, Brian, but ask yourself this: who am I going to bump into every day of the week here in Film City – Wes Clark or General Brandenburg?'

That evening was the first of many when we were joined at the bar by our US colleagues, with their newly arrived one star quite properly leading from the front.

Time seemed to pass incredibly quickly and in spite of everything a degree of order gradually emerged from the chaos that had been Kosovo when we arrived. With the assistance of a combination of military and civilian expertise, everything from ancient coal-fired power stations to water supplies, sanitation, prisons and air traffic control started to come back to life. On the law and order front we were very pleased to welcome legal and policing specialists working under the direction of the UNMIK SRSG[15] – first the Brazilian Sergio de Mello[16] and then his French successor, Bernard Kouchner – relieving soldiers and their commanders of the unfamiliar headache of those duties.

Before I knew it, my tour of duty was coming to a close but before I left, I had one final email exchange with the dreaded AFSouth which contained some very kind words from them and added a warm glow of satisfaction in a job which perhaps hadn't been so badly done after all. I was quite surprised at their generous comments, in view of our sometimes rather fractious relationship and felt a little guilty; perhaps at times I had been unduly harsh in my own assessment of my American comrades further up the chain of command.

With the end of an operational military deployment comes the uniquely sharp contrast of returning to the safety and comfort of home, from a time and place combining the possibility of death or injury, with the only certainty being uncertainty even for those of us flying a desk. Not since the last days of my first term at boarding school at the tender age of 8 had I felt such a delicious agony of anticipation. There had been moments of great excitement as well as of fear, stress and anxiety but certainly never a dull moment and, as I took off from Pristina for the last time, I reflected that for all the joy of returning home I certainly wouldn't have missed the whole experience for the world.

NATO was and remains a formidable organization but without the right leadership on the ground no amount of its political hype can guarantee a happy ending when the operational rubber hits the tactical road. General Jackson had achieved a fantastic outcome in Kosovo, to rival the achievements in their time of Wellington at Waterloo[17] and Woodward in the Falklands.

If this appears to be an exaggeration, the reader might try to imagine the ground war in Central Europe in the closing months of the twentieth century which would have ensued in the absence of a negotiated settlement. He had achieved this by a combination of personal charisma, strength and diplomacy which deserve a place forever in FCO training, never mind Staff College, with the patience of Job and military skills borne out of decades of experience. He wrapped it up with generosity and appreciation for those supporting him in HQ KFOR, including the warm goodbye he wished me as I left.

Chapter 5

ARRC Revisited

Having left Kosovo for JHQ in July 1999, I returned with my family from Germany to the UK in August. Despite my initially feeling a bit out of my depth, the ARRC had been a happy posting for all of us, albeit the challenges and excitement for me on deployment were mirrored by a degree of anxiety for the family left behind. Our eagerness at going home after nearly three years away was mixed with much regret at leaving Germany, possibly for the last time.

George Formby sang, 'You'll get no promotion this side of the ocean', but any soldier who has the opportunity to 'walk the walk' on an operational deployment stands a much better chance. I had never been particularly ambitious, a trait requiring political nous in the armed forces as in any other walk of life, which was by no means ever a talent of mine. I had ended up with NATO almost by accident but, sure enough, thanks largely to General Jackson's kind words in my subsequent annual report, I was promoted to colonel a few months after returning home.

The army, like the Almighty, 'moves in mysterious ways its wonders to perform' and much to my surprise, almost exactly ten years after my departure from my first ARRC tour I found myself back at JHQ again. The legal office at the HQ had undergone various upheavals over the years, one result being that the senior post had been upgraded to colonel, hence the opportunity for my second innings.

Arriving once again in January, this time I drove from the UK through some of the heaviest snow for many years. As luck would have it there was now a strong probability that we would be going to Afghanistan in the near future and the second preoccupation in the headquarters that winter was relocation later in the year back to the UK. The short stay in Germany did not warrant a family move, so I stayed in the mess, with my terrier Gnippa[1] for company.

The stage may have been familiar but I found myself amongst an entirely new cast. COMARRC was now Lieutenant-General Sir Richard

Shirreff, who greeted me warmly as we knew each other from HQ Land Command back in Wilton, where we had been on the staff together a few years earlier – and we even shared birthdays, to the year. The new chief of staff, Major-General Tim Evans, a wiry ex-special forces bundle of energy who looked impossibly young for his rank, was also a friendly face from earlier days. The combination of this familiarity with the commanders, and my own higher rank and experience meant I immediately felt comfortable and confident in this old stamping ground, unlike the trepidation of the first time round.

Our planned deployment to Afghanistan was still some twelve months away when I arrived but I found the ARRC every bit as manic with 'urgent' staff work as in the past. Quite apart from the more obvious contrasts between planning to go to Kabul rather than Kosovo, one major difference was that on this occasion we had real-time insight into what to expect, joining an operation which had already been ongoing for nearly a decade instead of trying to plan for one which might not even have happened at all. The schizophrenia last time round had been between exercise scenarios ('ARRCADE Fusion') and actual developments in Kosovo, and this time it was between the logistics of relocating to Gloucestershire and planning for an operational tour in Afghanistan.

As part of my own planning, I attended another LOAC course at the NATO school in the picturesque Oberammergau, Bavaria, familiar to me from previous NATO days. One reason I was particularly keen to attend this time was that the course would also be attended by Colonel Walt Hudson, the US JAG Corps colonel with whom I would be working in Kabul. He was a very experienced officer who had served in Iraq, Korea and Panama but always just in US formations, so NATO was new to him.

I met Walt on day one of the course and was really delighted to find him an enormously friendly and enthusiastic character. It was especially important that we got on since he would run the office in Kabul, at the insistence of the US, who would after all be commanding the headquarters as well as providing the majority of the staff. Walt was actually younger than me and I had been a colonel a while longer than him so we both might have found the situation a little awkward had we not hit it off.

I was intrigued to be assured with great authority by one of the 'professors' on the course that as a NATO soldier you would never be deployed on an operation in a foreign country without properly protected legal status. I could not resist pointing out the situation of Brits in FYROM back in 1999 but despite listening politely, I don't think she quite believed what I was telling her.

On day two we were assigned to discussion groups of about eight students. I led one group, and our instructions were that we needed to identify a non-native English speaker as syndicate spokesman to present our solution to the problem under discussion to the plenary course the following day. This was because the English speakers normally tended to hog the limelight and deprive others of the opportunity to speak up. We departed to our syndicate room but one officer was missing, an American pilot who arrived about ten minutes late, hugely apologetic, having had some unavoidable delay.

Spotting an opportunity, I said: 'That's absolutely fine; in fact, you've solved a problem for me.'

'How's that, sir?'

'By turning up late you've self-selected as our non-native English-speaking presenter tomorrow.'

At first, he thought I was kidding but although I had no problem with his late arrival and the atmosphere was perfectly good humoured, I stuck to my guns and he entered fully into the spirit.

The next morning our USAF friend stood up on stage when it came to our syndicate's turn: 'Before I explain what our syndicate has decided, I just wanted to begin by thanking Colonel Nelson for this great opportunity to practise and improve my English.'

Good for him – who said Americans don't understand irony?

The departure from JHQ was very sad. Many of the other nations were more than happy to relocate to the UK but for the Brits it just meant the end of an era and one more avenue for itchy-footed soldiers and their families to see a bit of the world closed off, quite apart from unfavourable comparisons between the spacious environment of JHQ and the semi-suburban former RAF Innsworth, Gloucester, which was to be our new home. The legal branch was spared any substantial involvement in the boring logistical details of the move but the final grand parade, with the Princess Royal taking the salute, followed by a rather subdued cocktail party, was a three-line whip.

The Bundeswehr also treated us to a farewell in the form of a traditional 'Grand Tattoo', or *Grosser Zapfenstreich*, its highest military ceremony, a rather Gothic torch-lit evening military band parade originally performed by the Prussian army in 1838 in honour of Tsar Nicholas I.

Gazela Shoe Factory, Skopje, North Macedonia – HQ KFOR, March–June 1999.

Refugee camp, North Macedonia, April 1999.

KFOR Tactical HQ, Pristina, Kosovo, June 1999.

Left: Legal Branch HQ KFOR, Pristina, July 1999. From left: Maj Bart Haverman (NL), Capt Jo Bowen ALS (UK), the author, Maj Brian Palmer USMC (JAG).

Below: Film City (aka 'Planet Hollywood'), HQ KFOR from June 1999.

NATO bomb damage, Kosovo, 1999.

Above left: A cheerful greeting at Kabul International Airport (KAIA).

Above right: KAIA, 2011.

HQ ISAF, formerly Kabul Sports Club, 2011.

Above: Legal Branch, HQ ISAF Joint Command July 2011 (the author is fifth from the right).

Left: Afghanistan, 'Land of dust', 2011.

Camp Bastion, Helmand, Afghanistan, October 2011. From left: Lt-Col Nigel Heppenstall ALS (UK Detention Oversight Team), the author, Maj John Harris ALS (UK Joint Force Support).

The author with 'bodyguard', FOB Salerno, December 2011.

Regional Command West, Herat, Afghanistan September 2011.

Targeting Roadshow, Herat, September 2011.

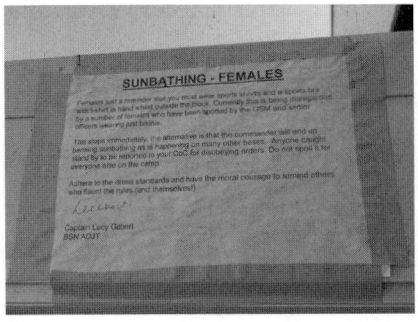 

Above left: 'The fun police' notice, Camp Bastion, 2011.

Above right: Drill training, Afghan National Army recruits, FOB Salerno, Khost Province, Afghanistan, December 2011.

Above: Medal parade. ISAF personnel assemble for NATO Non-Article V operational medal award ceremony.

Left: Pay parade. Hopeful compensation claimants in the street outside ISAF HQ, Kabul.

Above: ISAF Joint Command complex, KAIA, December 2011.

Right: IJC Mongolian contingent feeling at home in the snow, KAIA, December 2011.

IJC Legal Branch, 'the swamp', KAIA, 2011.

Christmas in Kabul, 2011.

Soon after our return to the UK, General Shirreff moved on to SHAPE as the four-star Deputy SACEUR and was succeeded as COMARRC by Lieutenant-General James Bucknall, whose grandfather had himself been a corps commander during the Second World War.

In the legal branch we no longer had a Dutchman but I was joined by a British major, Lee Burney, and later by an Italian lieutenant-colonel, Pietro d'Andrea, who looked uncannily like Super Mario, and was a charming, friendly colleague but sadly his English was almost non-existent.

I have no idea how Pietro slipped through the net, as English is NATO's lingua franca and it is supposed to have strict standards for officers' English language ability, but whatever the truth of the matter it was not right for our HQ to have to carry anybody with this disadvantage and also extremely unfair on the poor guy himself. Diplomacy dictated that we had to manage, so we found various ways of keeping Pietro out of trouble, but it was clear to me from the outset that there was no way we could take him with us on the operation.

At least now we had made the move, we could concentrate fully on the more exciting business of the operational deployment and we settled happily enough into our new office and stepped up our pre-deployment training, beginning with some history revision.

The Taliban government of Afghanistan, having refused to hand over Osama bin Laden to the US (ostensibly in accordance with the *Pashtunwali* code of honour), following the events of 9 September 2001, had been rapidly and forcibly ousted in early 2002 by the US in coalition with the UK and the 'Northern Alliance' of Mujahideen warlords. Later that same year, following the Bonn conference under UN auspices, a 'puppet' president, Hamid Karzai, had been installed at the head of the Government of the Islamic Republic of Afghanistan (GIROA). At the same time the International Security Assistance Force was established to suppress the rump of the Taliban and sundry like-minded extremist Islamist insurgents and enable a smooth transition to democratic government, to prevent the country ever again becoming a secure launchpad for the likes of Al-Qaeda against the West.

ISAF, run by NATO under command of a US four-star general with a British deputy, had got off to a reasonably promising start but at around the time the US, in particular, took their eye off the ball in 2003 in order to invade Iraq, things started to go badly wrong. In previous years

Afghanistan had endured the Soviet occupation, followed by the equally volatile regimes of the Mujahideen and then the Taliban. However, despite thousands more casualties suffered on all sides over the ISAF years, it was difficult to discern much improvement in the country's prospects by 2010, when the ARRC were preparing to deploy. This was not particularly surprising, given that Russia's withdrawal in 1989, after a decade of heavy casualties, is sometimes credited with marking the beginning of the end of the USSR, setting a greatly encouraging precedent for the Taliban and others resisting ISAF.

Having ballooned over the years, ISAF by now comprised military elements of varying shapes and sizes from at least fifty nations, the lion's share being US, but with a significant UK force in Helmand province, one of the areas most heavily fought over. Until 2009 ISAF operations had been run entirely from the four-star HQ in Kabul, located in what had been the Kabul Sports Club, with no interface between that level and the brigade-level regional commands under different national leads throughout the country.

This had left a crucial gap between the difficult politico-strategic business conducted between capitals and the bloody tactical realities faced by soldiers on the ground. The military solution was to create an intermediate three-star 'operational' headquarters, looking downwards and inwards, instead of up and out, in order to provide better direction and support to the regional commands. This new headquarters, known as the ISAF Joint Command (IJC) was established within the perimeter of Kabul International Airport (KAIA), whose principal traffic during these troubled times was either military or humanitarian relief rather than commercial.[2] IJC was originally intended to number a staff of fewer than a thousand but by the time the ARRC arrived to assume its core appointments in 2011, the numbers had swollen to more than double that and the infrastructure was at full stretch.

Every nation with even modest military capabilities, however loosely allied to the US and UK diplomatic effort in central Asia, wanted a piece of the action; it looked good politically, and soldiers everywhere relish the opportunity for some operational experience, not to mention operational pay. US servicemen all served at least twelve-month tours and paid no income tax while deployed. The Australians also enjoyed a generous deal and even we Brits were now catching up, with a healthy operational allowance. The penny packets of miscellaneous nations' armed forces were dotted all over the country in the regional commands and higher headquarters.

There were New Zealand special forces units, unexpected from such a small country but very effective, a Japanese unit, uniquely overseas since the Second World War, a Mongolian platoon, and even good old FYROM was there, providing the guard force at HQ ISAF. KAIA boasted an 'international military police force' commanded by COMKAIA, a Romanian Air Force brigadier or 'fleet commander'. His appointment was 'Chief of International Military Police', or 'Chimp' to the more facetious among us.[3]

The willingness of all these nations to put their money where their mouth was, and their unity of effort, were impressive but it could also tend to make the whole operation rather more unwieldy and complex than necessary, with 20 per cent of the staff doing 80 per cent of the work and the remainder milling around rather aimlessly.

The appointment of Chief of Staff, IJC, was 'flagged' to the UK (so our General Evans was to occupy that post). One of his predecessors in the early days in IJC had become particularly exasperated by the exponential growth in numbers at KAIA and decided something must be done.

By comparing the log-in records of people arriving for breakfast in either of the two enormous dining facilities (DFacs) with log-ins at people's work stations on the same morning, the COS identified dozens who were evidently on site simply consuming rations rather than contributing to the war effort. Each nation with personnel in theatre boasted a senior national representative (SNR) so the general summoned the IJC SNRs for all those identified as merely passengers and demanded that they be repatriated within the week. This seemed to be an end to the matter, with a useful reduction in numbers and a more streamlined headquarters as a result.

However, sadly for the general, it was not to be, because within minutes of receiving this unwelcome instruction every one of those SNRs was on the phone complaining loudly to their embassy. Sure enough, one by one each nation protested in turn to HQ ISAF, which promptly rescinded the marching orders. The bottom line was that it was deemed preferable to have too many people in theatre, despite the serious security risk faced by all ISAF personnel, the unnecessary consumption of money and life support and the constant strain on infrastructure and logistics, than to risk upsetting sending state governments by repatriating surplus people.

None of these realities on the ground were yet apparent to us back in sleepy Gloucestershire and few of the ARRC staff due to deploy had any previous experience in the Afghan theatre of operations. By now we had seen so many presentations on every aspect of the Afghan operational theatre that we just wanted to get on with it. There is only so much information which anyone could take on board about 'transition' (the process which was supposed to be happening out there to restore governance to the Afghans), poppy harvesting statistics, *Pashtunwali*, or the rule of law (or rather lack of it) in Helmand province. Fortunately, however, there were various more practical training events planned, the first of which was 'key leader training' for all colonels and above, who would be going on a recce to Kabul.

In late September 2010 about two dozen of us flew first to Dusseldorf, where we were met by a coach, for a couple of nights' stay near Brunssum, in Holland, home to a NATO HQ Allied Joint Force Command (AJFC). Since nothing is simple in NATO the ISAF chain of command goes up via AJFC to SHAPE. Hence, we were entertained there with a full day of 'death by PowerPoint' presentations, on a wide variety of aspects of current ISAF operations. Disappointingly, although the setting was new, almost none of the material was, which perhaps should not have surprised us, given NATO's tendency for overkill in such preparation.

Then it was literally back on the bus, this time to the nearby Geilenkirchen airbase where we embarked on a C-17 for Kabul, or so we thought. We were a little surprised to find within about fifteen minutes of take-off that we were already descending, as the pilot announced that we had an (unspecified) technical issue and we would be landing at yet another NATO airbase. After a couple of hours in Ramstein, Bavaria, which seemed more like a large US shopping mall than a military installation – indeed there was some suspicion that that was the true reason for the pilot's diversion – the technical issue was apparently fixed and we were off again, finally arriving at Bagram Air Base near Kabul three days after leaving Innsworth.

With a second runway added by the US in 2006, Bagram is an enormous facility originally built in the 1950s, used extensively by the USSR during their occupation of the country, partly destroyed since then during the Mujahideen era, and now occupied principally by USAF units of the US national Afghan operation 'Resolute Support'. There was even an Afghan Air Force presence there, limited almost entirely to a number of Russian Hip and Hind helicopters, of questionable reliability. It lies about twenty-five miles from Kabul and a road trip there would have been fascinating but we were a senior bunch, so security dictated that we were ferried over to HQ ISAF in a small fleet of US Black Hawk helicopters.

As the capital of the country at the heart of the nineteenth-century 'Great Game', Kabul was a name which for me, like a lot of people had always conjured up a rather exotic image. During more peaceful times, which historically never seem to last long in these parts, it had been a highly sought-after posting for diplomats and others, with grand palaces, luxuriant irrigated gardens, thriving bazaars and, at an altitude exceeding 1,500 metres, an ideal climate, at least in the summer.

Subsequently it became an essential staging post on the overland hippy trail between the west and the equally exotic Katmandu. Sadly, as I was now about to see for myself, those happier days are long past, with the combination of years of war, overcrowding and the pollution which accompanies it turning a once relaxed and exciting city into an insecure, rubbish-strewn and chaotic rabbit warren.

It was a place which until recent years I would never have dreamt of visiting on a military mission. All that changed overnight on 'nine eleven' of course and I recall within days of those events joking with an ALS colleague who had recently seriously upset the management, 'It'll be Legal Branch Kabul for you next then, David.' And to the amazement of both of us, that's exactly what happened to him a matter of a few months later, when he was dispatched on about the same day John Simpson 'liberated' the city.

The last thing I had expected was to end up here too, but now it was my turn, as we swooped over the mud-built compounds of Kabul's suburbs with the foothills of the Hindu Kush in the background, before touching down on the sports pitch at HQ ISAF. As I looked out of my window the following morning, I could see those mountaintops surrounding Kabul were now blanketed with the first snows of the autumn. They looked spectacular and I remarked to my roommate that although our briefings had repeatedly insisted that Afghanistan was in such a state that there was no ambition to 'turn it into Switzerland overnight', that was exactly what appeared to have just happened.

The next day we were introduced to the legendary General David Petraeus, Commander ISAF and Commander, US forces in Afghanistan.

As a four-star general with a reputation earnt in Iraq as the world's military expert in counterinsurgency or COIN operations, this appointment was for him the pinnacle of a stellar military career. He had just left the army to become Director of the CIA when I began my tour in Kabul the following year, and the year after that he resigned, following the disclosure of an extra-marital affair.

We then spent yet another morning of PowerPoint, much of it identical to what we had now already received in conference rooms in several other countries. The main difference here appeared to be in the complexity of some of the slides, which were literally wiring diagrams to make a nuclear physicist proud but absolutely no use to man nor beast in illustrating anything useful. In the right hands PowerPoint – which we were largely spared in Kosovo, and remarkably managed quite well without, before Microsoft had conquered the world – is a great tool, but not when used for support rather than illumination, like a drunk uses a lamppost.

The HQ ISAF compound was in the centre of the so-called Kabul Green Zone, a supposedly impenetrable secure area, surrounded by a 'ring of steel' of barricades and police checkpoints, which also housed a number of embassies and the large US Camp Eggers, home to the NATO Training Mission Afghanistan (NTMA). It was a sprawling establishment of Hesco blast barriers, hastily erected prefabricated office and accommodation blocks, communications equipment, the sports pitch turned helipad, and carparks full of heavily armoured Land Cruisers, Chevy Suburbans and APCs. The original Kabul Sports Club building was a remnant of the elegant city of earlier times, an attractive pink and yellow palace now containing the commander's inner sanctum, opposite which was the lawned 'Rose Garden', which accommodated one of a number of snack bars dotted around the compound.

At one time you could enjoy a cold beer on a warm evening in the Rose Garden but this had all come to an end under the regime of Petraeus's predecessor, the 'Warrior Monk' General McChrystal.[4] Legend had it that when he summoned a staff meeting late one night in September 2009 to deal with an airstrike crisis which had killed scores of civilians, McChrystal found a number of his officers the worse for drink and ordered the closure of the bar forthwith.

After much waiting around in the afternoon, we eventually donned body armour, helmets and goggles to embark in the Black Hawks up to KAIA to visit the jumble of IJC buildings clustered around a gymnasium which had been turned into the Joint Operations Centre. I met the US JAG Corps officers, who seemed pleased to have a visitor, in the legal office where I would be working in due course with their successors, and which reminded me of a cross between a large chicken shed and the Korean 'Swamp' occupied by Hawkeye, Trapper and Frank Burns in *M.A.S.H.* It did not lack atmosphere but I thought at the time, and continued to worry in later months, that the place would go up like a bonfire in the event of an attack.

Rommel had it absolutely right: 'Time spent in reconnaissance is seldom wasted' and for me this trip up to IJC was by far the most useful element of the recce. From then on, I had in my mind's eye the physical working environment that no amount of clever slides could have replicated. Those wiring diagrams with their 'metrics' of how many IEDs had gone off, how many insurgents had been detained or how much poppy had been destroyed in X or Y province went in one ear and out the other, and would be even more meaningless by the time we actually arrived in theatre.

The return trip spared us the PowerPoint pitstops of the outward journey but was equally unconventional. With KAIA situated at such a high altitude, the little military C-160[5] turboprop in which we embarked was unable to get airborne during the heat of the day, so we had to take off at an uncivilized 4 am to claw our way up above the mountains towards the northwest.

First stop about two hours later was the military section of the airport at Dushanbe, a name which had meant nothing to me but which we learnt was the capital of Tajikistan. Sadly all we got to see on the ground was yet more snow-covered hills.

The French military operated the base and immediately on arrival we were surrounded by forklift trucks offloading freight, driven by muscular, tattooed, skinhead airmen from L'Armee de l'air. They were dressed in skin-tight camouflaged shorts and T-shirts as if for a Village People concert, and appeared to be just taking a rare break from a tour of duty otherwise spent entirely in the gym. We were there in the transit terminal just long enough to enjoy coffee and patisseries worthy of the Promenade des Anglais, before embarking on the next leg in a very smart Belgian Air Force Embraer executive jet.

I settled down expecting a comfortable flight back at least as far as Brussels, only to find we were landing yet again after just another couple of hours, this time descending over the Caspian Sea into Baku, capital of Azerbaijan, for a refuelling stop, apparently retracing the Silk Road by air. Then it was another mystery hop, this time landing back in Geilenkirchen. Speculation there as to how and when we were eventually meant to find our way back to Innsworth was resolved by the arrival of a very boring and unglamorous bus, on which we eventually got home, exhausted, via the Channel Tunnel roughly twenty-four hours after leaving Kabul.

The ARRC's deployment to IJC was fixed to begin in January 2011. Some senior officers would serve a twelve-month tour, US style, for continuity, but most of us would serve for one of two back-to-back six month 'rotations'. The IJC legal office would be staffed principally by US JAG personnel, reflecting the US command and numbers within the headquarters, with two UK posts shared by the army with the Royal Navy and the RAF. We split the ARRC legal deployment so that my major, Lee Burney, would be on the first rotation so he could earn his medal before posting out of the ARRC and I would replace him in July for the second six months. Pietro was content to man the office in the rear, sparing us any embarrassing diplomatic dispute about the decision not to send him.

Principal mission rehearsal exercises in NATO are conducted at the Joint Warfare Centre, Stavanger, where Lee duly attended for a fortnight in the autumn of 2010. However, the command of IJC was due to be assumed by the US I Corps the following summer, coinciding roughly with our second rotation. They were based at Fort Lewis, Seattle, and it was decided that it would make better sense all round for our mission rehearsal to be conducted there. The prospect of spending some time sampling US hospitality at the largest army base on the west coast was a lot more exciting than chilly Norway, so this idea, which was fixed for April 2011, suited us all very well.

This time the travel was remarkably straightforward: a scheduled BA 747 flight direct from Heathrow to Seattle. Better still, when I presented my boarding pass the stewardess tore it up and replaced it with one which involved turning left, a rare treat. I later discovered that I had been the senior officer on that particular flight and the 'movements' major responsible had kindly allocated me a wild card among our seat reservations. I travelled in great style and slept for much of the flight but when I woke up just before landing my right foot was really painful, and I could barely walk. Having hobbled my way through arrivals and been collected and driven to my accommodation, I decided to suffer in silence overnight and hope the relentless throbbing would resolve itself by morning.

The following day, when the exercise was due to begin first thing, matters were no better and I was starting to worry that I might have a deep vein thrombosis. I was reminded on arrival at the exercise centre how the US always do things on a grand scale. It was a smart, dedicated hi-tech complex, purpose built for this sort of exercise, a far cry from the draughty disused Ayrshire barracks in Monchengladbach of ARRCADE Confusion fame, and sure enough there was also a medical post right there where I needed one.

On presenting myself, I was immediately surrounded by uniformed medics who bundled me into an ambulance bound for the base hospital. I was used to army medical centres in little more than Nissen huts in UK but the Fort Lewis equivalent was about the size of the Royal Free. The medics were clearly very concerned not to kick off this visit by a large contingent of Brits with a senior serious casualty, so I spent literally all morning being minutely examined by paramedics and doctors ranging from warrant officers to colonels.

In the end, despite all this high-powered, sophisticated scanning and prodding, the diagnosis, which would undoubtedly have cost something in four figures in a civilian US hospital, was inconclusive and I was despatched with two bottles of pills (even the pills are supersized in the States) and advised to 'take it easy and see if these do any good'. I discovered that one bottle was good old Ibuprofen but after a day or so on the others, which were so powerful that they must have been some sort of horse tranquilizer – bringing on the most euphoric dreams – all was well.

I never did find out what my mystery ailment was but clearly it was nothing serious; I suspect maybe a touch of gout brought on by a combination of high altitude and complimentary British Airways Moët. Anyway, I made a point of hanging on to the horse tranquilizers, to be savoured as morale medication should things turn ugly during the deployment.

On putting in my belated appearance on the exercise, I was greeted like an old friend by Walt Hudson, who commanded the I Corps Judge Advocate's 'shop', the biggest JAG office in the US army, with dozens of military lawyers and paralegals under his command; in fact, his one office equated to about half the numbers in the entire UK army legal service. Walt immediately made me feel welcome and introduced me to the other legal officers selected to join him on the deployment. He had decided to 'max out' the numbers in order to give as many as possible from his branch the operational experience. I had some reservations about this, particularly having seen the limited office accommodation available in theatre but it was his show and not a good idea to get off on the wrong foot by questioning this proposal.

The exercise, led by a team detached from Afghanistan whose familiarity with all the current issues was invaluable, passed quickly and despite the inevitable dreaded PowerPoint interludes, we learnt a lot. In the legal office such issues as rules of engagement (which were a priority from the top down, in contrast to Kosovo), targeting, with particular reference to collateral damage, and detention kept us heavily preoccupied.

My return trip was pain free and once back in Gloucestershire, we only had a couple of months before the real thing, a period of frenetic, last-minute preparation, medical certification and finally, packing.

Departure date was Wednesday, 27 July, I was up at 4.30 am for a roll call and departure by coach from Imjin Barracks to the Joint Services Air Mounting Centre at South Cerney to be reunited with baggage, eat breakfast, complete security procedure and hang about aimlessly for a couple of hours. I met up there with Lieutenant-Colonel Cathy Braddick-Hughes, an old friend and colleague from ALS, who was due to serve alongside me up at KAIA.

Then it was back on the bus for about an hour's trip east to RAF Brize Norton, which I had first visited some thirty-seven years earlier en route to Hong Kong. The bus was packed, with Bergen rucksacks perched uncomfortably on our knees. Surrounded by slightly nervous chatter, it seemed a little surreal to be meandering through the leafy Cotswold countryside but at least I had some idea of what to expect at the other end following the recce the previous year.

The advantage of the diversion via South Cerney instead of going straight to Brize was that unlike the bad old days of sitting around in an overcrowded and uncomfortable terminal for half a day, with RAF movements staff relishing their temporary control over their bored and frustrated army 'rivals', we drove straight out to the aircraft.

The C-17 took off dead on time at 1200 midday for an unremarkable seven-hour flight, wearing body armour for the last hour or so in Afghan airspace.

Chapter 6

Welcome to Kabul

We landed at 10 pm local time, three and a half hours ahead of UK time and stepped down from the aircraft into a warm, dusty evening, feeling for a moment like excited holidaymakers escaping a mediocre British summer for guaranteed warmer climes. Looking around, the dim outline of the mountains visible against the night sky on all sides added to the feeling of adventure but we were reminded that this was not in fact a holiday destination by the rows of parked military helicopters and US Air National Guard C-130s surrounding us, without an EasyJet or TUI in sight.

The entrance to the terminal, with its 'Welcome to Kabul' sign above the doors was framed somewhat incongruously by large sculptures of an eagle on one side and a bear on the other, gifts from their respective nations, no doubt intended to remind US and German servicemen that they were not forgotten as they arrived on deployment. From the scrum of a dozen different nations' combat uniforms, I soon spotted Walt with a broad grin on his face; he had been on the ground for several weeks now and kindly made a point of greeting me despite the late hour. There was also a beaming Lee Burney, for whom my arrival meant his own home time had finally also arrived, although flight delays meant it would take him another frustrating ten days to get out.

I was then swept up by a brisk and efficient Geordie warrant officer, who grabbed my bags and led me confidently past the queue of soldiers awaiting documentation checks, through the 'land' side of the terminal to a waiting 4x4. I was hot and tired, so this small example of the benefit of being one pip senior than my last time in NATO made all the difference at such a time, as I was in my new bunk within an hour of landing while others were still wrestling with military bureaucracy. Sleep was slow to come though, my mind whirring and body confused by the altered time zone, but I eventually succumbed, in the slightly smug knowledge that I was now the most senior serving British military lawyer ever to deploy on an operational tour outside Europe.[1]

The first few days were spent in acclimatization in every sense. First, my roommate introduced himself: Colonel René Pals, the senior Dutch officer on the HQ staff, a very pleasant, quiet artillery officer, who, naturally, spoke perfect English and turned out to be an ideal companion in the circumstances, as he kept similar working hours to me and, most importantly, never snored.

The accommodation comprised a small ground floor room with two double bunks, but with just the two of us in it, providing a bit of spare space for kit, a small desk and chair for each of us and communal ablutions down the corridor. Everything was constantly covered in a not-so-thin layer of dust but we counted ourselves lucky to be a little way out of the heavily polluted city. Many people ended up in very basic transit accommodation for a short while on arrival which would have been a pain but my only move was halfway through the tour, when I got back from R&R to find my room empty. We had been moved to a newly built block and dear old René had moved all my kit for me as well as his own.

This had the advantage of being on the first floor and nearer the perimeter fence, thereby leaving behind the noisy diesel trucks revving up outside the window in the early mornings. We had a great view of the mountains which were spectacularly snowy in winter, making me want to go skiing, but we were in earshot of the nearest muezzin, just to remind us in the early hours of the morning that this was nowhere near the Alps.

Some nations, like the Aussies, had negotiated expensive deals to secure entire accommodation blocks for their own people, with single rooms, 'residents' lounge', gym and all the trimmings. Others also flocked together in their own enclaves, such as the French, who manned the main medical facility, the Romanians and the Mongolians, and of course the various special forces units either were, or at least considered themselves to be, far too elite and sneaky beaky to mix with ordinary mortals.

Construction work was constantly going on, as, far from shrinking, the overcrowded headquarters still seemed to be sucking in ever more staff, but once built, the maintenance of the place ground to a halt because the central budget stopped there, and getting individual nations then to fund upkeep was like trying to build the tower of Babel. The infrastructure suffered from excessive wear and often struggled to cope, not helped by largely idle locally employed maintenance and cleaning staff whose long breaks for the likes of Ramadan,[2] Eidh or seemingly weekly national holidays often left such jobs undone for weeks on end, sometimes leading to unpleasant sanitary and gastric consequences.

There were no bars, because the dreaded US General Order No. 1 had found its way up here, applying to all nations, with dire consequences threatened for infringements, although adherence still varied. In fact, there was no social life as such in this very basic accommodation but neighbouring faces soon became familiar. In my case, for example, we had a very interesting Lithuanian colonel just down the corridor for whom this was the second tour in Afghanistan, his first having been as a captain based at Mazar I Sharif with the Soviet army in the 1980s – what a contrast he was seeing (or was it?).

Interspersed among the accommodation blocks was a complete mix of commercial enterprises. There was an excellent laundry service which rapidly turned around a massive load of kit, really only wearable for one day because of the heat and dirt. A tagged bagging system ensured you (almost) always got your own stuff back, which was just as well because once lost it was gone forever unless you were willing to spend an afternoon rifling through an unhygienic pile of other people's smalls. Beyond that, there was a pretty good Thai restaurant, a couple of juice bars, a barber-cum-salon doing a roaring trade for yet another Thai enterprise and various PX sources of tax-free electronic goods and sports kit.

A fairly substantial hospital was the domain of the large number of French personnel seen wandering about. I later learnt that this facility was to be avoided, as there were rumours of somewhat unorthodox and presumably painful techniques concerning the administration of fluids via an unusual orifice, and drips being allowed to run dry overnight. Walking past the hospital one evening, I was amused to see a patient sitting on a bench with a drip stand in front of him, all plumbed into his arm, while savouring a cigarette, simultaneous intravenous and oral medication – only in France, surely!

On the one occasion I did attend for a routine consultation at 9 am I gave up waiting, as the coffee-brewing, logging on and staff morning kisses on both cheeks was still going on an hour later but nothing else was happening. I went next door to a US facility where I was dealt with immediately.

The Afghans also ran a bazaar of sorts in a corner of the camp, undoubtedly the most expensive in the capital because it was largely patronized by overpaid US soldiers who, a few weeks before tour's end would invariably treat themselves to a shopping spree. Rather like that famous scene from Monty Python's *Life of Brian*, however, the notion of haggling was not an American forte; top dollar was affordable and the bazaar tradesmen knew it.

Thousands of dollars would be spent on large consignments of Persian and Afghan carpets, carved wooden chests, shawls and bric-a-brac, packed up and shipped home in advance. Unfortunately, this meant that although there were some very interesting and authentic items on display in amongst the knocked-off CDs and pink plastic muezzin alarm clocks, bargains were hard to come by, whatever the depth of your pocket.

The largest purpose-built constructions in this sprawling complex were the two dining facilities or 'DFacs', both of which succeeded in producing a remarkable variety of meals three times a day seven days a week. Much of the food came in via a regular 747 flight from Dubai, and the rest overland via Karachi. Now and again ISAF would upset the Pakistanis and the overland route would be blockaded for a few weeks, at which point the standard of catering did noticeably decline. There was quite a lot of whingeing about what was on offer, sadly often by our American colleagues for whom much of the diet was probably a bit too European, but apart from the occasional Pakistani interference I thought this was wholly unjustified, with terrific quality and variety, not to mention quantity, and always a cheery Afghan steward welcoming you at the door.

This did not prevent one US brigadier dropping himself in serious hot water by trying to circumvent these feeding arrangements. After he had been in headquarters for some months, it transpired that he had been signing weekly declarations to the effect that he and his branch of the HQ were serving in what Uncle Sam deemed a 'remote location', which entitled him to claim a special ration allowance for them all. A truck was regularly being dispatched, at some risk to the driver every time, to a US catering establishment somewhere in Kabul, returning with the requisite payload of burgers, fries, doughnuts, ice-cream and other US dietary essentials. This was clearly fraudulent, involving Walt in some legal gymnastics in advising Com IJC how to deal with this high-ranking offender.

For my taste we had plenty of good old American fare on offer anyway and one of the most tempting dietary novelties was of course their take on breakfast, with many starting their day with impossibly stacked helpings of pancakes and maple syrup, often tastefully supplemented with eggs and bacon on the same plate. Others would fill polystyrene 'oyster' containers to eat out in their workplace, an uncivilized practice to which I put a stop in our legal shack; none of us were so busy that we needed to do this, and the smell seemed to find its way into the wooden fabric of the office, lingering all day.

All this consumption had to be burnt off somehow and although a few addicted souls maintained a jogging habit, the route round and round inside the perimeter reminded me of caged animals in a zoo, so, like most people, I turned to the gym.

Throughout my career thus far I had never been tempted to become a 'gym bunny' but it was immediately obvious that if I was to share six months behind the wire with all those calories and not emerge twice my original weight, walking from bunk to DFAC to office and back again was not going to cut it. I made 'fizz'[3] a fixture in my daily routine. Some people clearly had very little to occupy their months in Kabul, spending much of their tour overdosing on 'get big' protein powder, on sale in camp in enormous containers like paint tins. They grimaced and grunted their way through the afternoons, pumping iron in front of the mirrors with which the interior of the gym was for some obscure reason lined. I never did get to understand why people need to work out in front of a mirror – some sort of narcissistic or homoerotic kick, I suppose.

Compromised by its rubberized inflatable construction, the gym's air conditioning struggled vainly in the summer months with the challenge of all those frantically iron-pumping, rowing, cycling, jogging and Zumba-ing soldiers. Consequently, it was often oppressively hot and sweaty, and shared with flies almost as big and noisy as some of the iron-pumpers. Nevertheless, I would sneak in quietly for my forty minutes on a rowing machine most afternoons, content to spend an hour out of the office with my iTunes while shedding a few DFAC pancakes, trying to avoid eye contact with some behemoth of a Belgian military policeman admiring the reflection of his own tattooed biceps.

With levels of air traffic on our side of the airport at a fraction of its design capacity, much of the terminal was taken up by our command team's offices, in many cases with views out across the runway towards the mountains which would have a Canary Wharf hedge fund magnate green with envy. The remaining staff were across the road, many in the

JOC, with row upon row of officers at desks festooned with comms paraphernalia, facing a huge split screen of CNN, VTC briefings and live feeds from all over Afghanistan and beyond, like a scene from Cape Canaveral launching a NASA moon shot.

Adjacent to this was the warren of jerry-built work spaces like our legal hut, to which we all became quite attached, although towards the end of my tour we moved into a soulless, shiny new ergonomic office. It just wasn't the same, because as lawyers we may not have been in the thick of the action but at least in the 'Swamp' you felt like a soldier on ops. The move felt like vacating a beamy thatched cottage full of period features for a boring Persimmon new build rabbit hutch.

The site was linked by a traffic circuit alive with every model of 4x4 imaginable, in most cases armoured, and all bristling with aerials denoting electronic countermeasure equipment, fitted to jam radio-controlled improvised explosive device (IED) signals.[4] Like the majority of the personnel at IJC the vehicles spent 90 per cent of their time inside the wire, occasionally venturing out cautiously in convoys of two or three for short essential journeys to other ISAF locations such as the HQ downtown. All this heavy kit crammed onto a small, cheaply constructed road network played havoc with the surface, especially in the winter when large potholes and puddles of slush awaited the unwary pedestrian on a dark evening.

The months of preparation which had preceded my arrival certainly paid off in the office, and unlike Kosovo days most of the issues to be worked on were familiar. It did not take long to find my way around my new home but inevitably there remained various 'in processing' matters to be completed within the first few days.

This entailed a trip out on the first afternoon to the nearby Camp Souter (named after Captain Thomas Souter, sole survivor of the Battle of Gandamak during the disastrous British retreat from Kabul in January 1842), for which, donning heavy body armour and armed with an assortment of Brownings and SA80 rifles, we trundled for forty-five minutes or so in half a dozen armoured 4x4s through streets so run down they made Katmandu look like Kensington. On arrival, we spent the day being reminded yet again of information on ISAF and Taliban activity, threat levels and forecasts. This was followed by some weapons training on the range, but the only local novelty was a demonstration of the use of the tourniquet which was part of our issued first-aid kit. This was a little depressing but the statistics of amputations carried out in the field were frightening, particularly in the US regional commands, where the average was about five per week and even though the prospects of IED attacks on staff in our neck of the woods were relatively slim, it was one item of practical training which very much focused the mind.

The combination of seriously hot weather and the previous day's flight out had me fighting a losing battle with fatigue before the end of the day and it was with enormous relief that I shed all the hot and heavy kit back in my bunk and, with barely the energy for a shower, I was then out cold for a good ten hours.

Once all these preliminaries were over, it was good to start settling into the working routine and to reacquaint myself with my US colleagues. There was Walt of course, his deputy, a lieutenant-colonel called Greg, four captains, a warrant officer, a sergeant and an Australian naval legal services lieutenant commander. My compatriot Cathy ended up being diverted to the four-star HQ where they had a vacancy, which was a good move, because like much of our headquarters the legal branch was clearly overstaffed, as I had predicted. Lee Burney spent a couple of days in the office with me, introducing me to the current issues on our desks which was very useful and then I sent him away to clear some space and pack and try to relax while hanging around for his delayed flight home.

Although the legal problems on our plate were well established, they were no less complex than in the Balkans, and played out here on a much grander scale. Perhaps the major strategic legal issue was the rule of law, in which a substantial amount of money and manpower was invested across the country by military and civilian personnel from many areas of expertise besides the lawyers.

A far more typical task for us as military lawyers was to advise on matters of targeting, itself roughly sub-divided into those human targets featuring in a deliberately compiled 'effects list' for either kill or capture, and both human and inanimate targets of opportunity. Woven into that already complex task were the ISAF rules of engagement which had to account not only for the vagaries of so many member nations but also the provisions of Afghan law and an unpredictable government.

This was all taking place in the context of 'transition', the process of handing off as much as possible and as soon as possible to the fragile Afghan National Security Forces (ANSF), as ISAF and the US in particular sought the exit door from a seemingly interminable, and many believed unwinnable, commitment. President Obama was to be seeking his second term of office during the following year so the US political commitment to draw down as rapidly as possible was well publicized.

Talk about history repeating itself; this reminded me of Kosovo days, when Clinton welcomed the distraction from his impeachment problems, and when, as the reader will recall, in order to keep every NATO member nation on side for the air campaign, it had been emphasized that there would be no ground war. Just as Milosevic took heart and was emboldened by that assurance, it was obvious that the Taliban would be encouraged in their campaigning by the knowledge that they only had to hold on a little longer and the enemy would be gone – hardly an incentive to weaken their resolve.

Meanwhile, besides targeting and the rule of law, the office dealt with a whole host of other business, much of which was US only. It was clear that Walt and his merry men should reserve advising on those national matters to themselves but that alone did not determine how he and I were to cooperate. Initially we thought I should take on rule of law while Walt ran everything else, as it could certainly fully occupy the time of a colonel within that headquarters.

However, it soon became clear that this would not work, mainly because the US JAG Corps had officers out on the ground throughout the country with the so-called 'Provincial Reconstruction Teams' who expected direction and coordination from a US officer. So, after a very few days we had a rethink and Walt took on rule of law as well as all US specific legal advice while I assumed the more administrative task of running all other business, and the office, in itself enough to keep me reasonably well occupied given our swollen ranks and the variety of other issues which came our way.

It was still easier said than done to persuade the hyper-energetic Walt to relinquish the tiller at all. Even when he was out of the office on one of his trips upcountry, he insisted on checking in every couple of hours in case he was missing something, or perhaps we weren't coping without him.[5]

Walt was a second-generation soldier, commissioned from the ultra-traditional Citadel[6] officer training academy in Charleston, South Carolina, his home state, and he combined total dedication to his duties as both US officer and lawyer with devout Catholicism. I later discovered he was also a knowledgeable country music fan, once rounding on one of the captains: 'You don't like Johnny Cash – what are you, a Communist!'

He inhabited a sort of cubbyhole at the back of the 'Swamp', a bit like Fagin's lair, where he settled down in the morning emitting long, loud and vulgar yawns for an hour or so, with a variety of additional sound effects once fully awake, throughout the rest of the day. These included loud demands for 'Chief' Ferrell, usually for some form of immediately vital IT assistance or complex travel reservation.

Russell 'Rusty' Ferrell, himself a former Apache helicopter pilot, was clearly devoted to Walt. He was a highly intelligent and likeable colleague, who despite his undoubted loyalty was not above the occasional insubordinate but very accomplished imitation of Walt for the entertainment of the office when he wasn't looking.

Walt was himself equally devoted to General Curtis Scaparotti, the three-star US I Corps' 'Commanding General'[7] (CG), and now also our CG at IJC. A phone call from his office would immediately have Walt leaping from his desk, cap wedged firmly on head, and striding for the door with a portentous 'Gotta go see Scap' – a fairly frequent occurrence which Rusty would reprise with great accuracy immediately the door had slammed behind the man on his war-winning mission.

Walt was very sensitive to the fact that although he ruled his roost up at KAIA, there was also down the road at HQ ISAF a JAG office to support the four-star COMISAF. We would quite frequently have visits from their staff but they were greeted with deep suspicion by our intrepid leader, especially if unannounced, who clearly feared we were being spied on.

That office was also run by a US JAG colonel, Mike Jordan, who was a super fit ball of energy in the Marines, and a close confidant of Petraeus.[8] He clearly enjoyed his status downtown and was not averse to winding Walt up at times. This sometimes resulted in loud and ill-tempered telephone calls, on one occasion Walt proclaiming: 'This could go all the way to the President' (cue much covert sniggering).

Another time Mike refused to disclose a legal advice to his general which Walt insisted 'Scap' also needed to see. The air was blue and the devout, clean-living Catholic was not happy: 'Who the f*** does that Marine bastard think he is!'

One morning not long after this, a slightly chastened Walt warned the office that he was concerned that the volume and profanity of our language in the legal office needed to be toned down. Given that we all knew who was the principal culprit, this admonition caused politely raised eyebrows all round, but he went on to explain, *sotto voce* that 'The padre's office is just through there', pointing at the flimsy back wall of his cubbyhole. Luckily Walt could see the humour in this, but we never did find out if there had actually been a canonical complaint or maybe just some funny looks over the Eucharist.

On five days a week the working routine began with the commander's 'stand up', a secure video conference presentation by HQ ISAF staff to the commander on the events of the previous twenty-four hours and a look ahead to the next, attended by every headquarters in the chain of command from SHAPE down to the one-star regional commands. This was an important tool for everyone's situational awareness and I would alternate listening duty for our office with Walt, noting and reporting back to the office on any issues which called for our action.

The standard and detail of presentations varied considerably, with the inevitable PowerPoint wiring diagrams to illustrate the various 'metrics' which obsessed the chain of command, such as the number and location of IED attacks, insurgents killed, captured or detained, friendly forces killed or wounded, quantity of heroin seized and area of poppy destroyed. Most presenters were American but they were interspersed with the odd slightly nervous non-native speaker, and General Allen, the recently installed successor to Petraeus, was invariably courteous and appreciative with his occasional comments or queries.

The tone was always positive and rightly so, but in reality, progress was usually difficult to discern, sometimes two steps forwards and one back but sadly often the opposite. In trying to make sense of the blizzard of statistics I was reminded of the old adage that 'You can't fatten a pig by weighing it', but it seemed a lot of the time the weighing was all we could do in this historically intractable theatre of operations.

Back in the office I was getting to know, and without exception like, my colleagues, who were a mixed bunch. Greg, Walt's second in command back home, was an unusually quiet and dry character for an American, another loyal fan of his boss and a thoroughly competent operator. We shared many morale-boosting chuckles about the ISAF predicament but there were also times during Walt's absences when I took over from him which exposed the differences between the British and American ways of doing this business.

Welcome to Kabul

The Aussie, Dave, was clever, outspoken, deliberately provocative and thoroughly entertaining. On one famous occasion I managed to switch the lights out on him in the loo, causing a minor accident. An enraged Australian voice demanded from a darkened cubicle: 'What stupid bastard turned the f***ing lights out?'

I immediately owned up and apologized, at which he laughed, 'No worries, colonel. I guess if that's the worst thing that happens to me out here, I can't complain.'

I also once overheard an exchange between him and a particularly 'tree-hugging' NGO rep in which they were discussing the infamous local practice often referred to as 'Man Love Thursday'. On the eve of the Islamic sabbath the blatant incidence in the Afghan Army of what would have been serious offences of paedophilia in other countries invariably peaked throughout the country, with offenders presumably believing in some form of immediate absolution by dint of their devotions in the mosque on the following day.

The NGO's view was that it was inappropriate 'moral relativism', and not for us interlopers to be judging, let alone criticizing or seeking to influence local customary norms. Dave's sense of mischief found this irresistible and he suggested with an innocuous smile that perhaps in that case we should also turn a blind eye to any instances of female genital mutilation which we might encounter. The NGO's response, once she had recovered from the choking fit, included language which is not repeatable here – I guess even moral relativism is all relative for some.

The captains were Chris, a Californian Berkeley University graduate and the brightest of the bunch, Andrew, a rufty-tufty Minnesotan, fiercely proud of his special forces brother, and never seen without body armour and M4 rifle, Katy, a national-standard javelin thrower from Texas and Jen, slightly older than the others, with a Washington DC legal background. Last but not least among the US team was Sergeant Seabaugh, a soldier turned lawyer who had tired of representing 'low life druggie douchebags' for the Public Defender's office back home also in Texas and was very happy to return to uniform as a non-commissioned paralegal. They were without exception keen as mustard and proud to have been selected from a sizeable cast for this, in many cases, their first operational deployment.

Enjoying a slightly elevated situation a short distance away from the city, our airport base felt reasonably secure but we were outside the so called 'ring of steel' which was supposed to guarantee security in Kabul city centre. In ISAF terms, Kabul was 'Regional Command Capital' (RCC), for which Turkey had provided much of the garrison from the outset, although France was the lead nation. The Turks were well chosen, being not only one of NATO's strongest and most effective armed forces but, as Muslims, enjoying a naturally more comfortable relationship than other national contingents with the locals, including the ANSF who were supposed to be doing all the heavy lifting in preparation for transition post-ISAF in 2014.

Nobody had much confidence in ANSF notions of security, compromised as it so often was by treachery, fear, corruption, threats, drug taking, laziness, general inefficiency or any combination of the above, and the ring of steel was repeatedly shown to be something of a joke, and serious breaches were sadly a regular fact of life.

On 19 August the Taliban decided to celebrate Independence Day[9] by launching a 'complex'[10] suicide attack inside the ring of steel on the British Council premises, a soft target resulting in eleven deaths including a New Zealand special forces soldier killed in the relief operation.

Tethered a couple of hundred feet above the centre of Kabul was an unusual landmark in the form of a barrage balloon, which provided the platform for a live CCTV feed into a monitor within the HQ ISAF JOC, playing all day but, like a boring square of wallpaper, ignored by everybody. However, at about 1 pm on 13 September, less than a month after the British Council attack, a US major on his way out to the DFAC for lunch, noticed something unusual on the screen out of the corner of his eye and paused for a closer look.

As he grasped what he was seeing his appetite rapidly vanished – 'Holy sh**!' – and his hand instinctively reached for the pistol in its smart leather holster on his right hip. What he had seen was a hail of small-arms fire incoming on his own HQ from a semi-constructed tower block just outside the perimeter, an attack unheard and unnoticed until then in the JOC, which was at the heart of the target.

Outside, however, the Macedonian and Canadian guard forces were furiously returning fire from sangars[11] on the perimeter, like something out of *Beau Geste*. The attack had already begun with an RPG attack on the nearby US embassy, hitting the USAID compound and the nearby Afghan MoD. All hell was let loose, with the Canadians running low on ammunition and some staff officers, seeing this as their one opportunity on the tour actually to fire a shot in anger, rushing to join in the defensive barrage. It took until the following morning, with the assistance of special forces and helicopter gun platforms to dislodge the determined attackers, killing thirty, but amazingly with no ISAF casualties.

Even up at KAIA we were still smelling and hearing the sounds of the siege for several hours, with our scratchy Tannoy furiously warning us to take cover, amid intelligence suggesting we were the next target. I was on the phone to Cathy in the HQ JAG office when I heard what sounded unmistakeably like machine-gun fire.

'What the hell's going on, Cathy?'

'We're under attack at the minute' were her immortal and remarkably nonchalant words. There were rumours that the insurgents had breached the perimeter and were on the loose within HQ ISAF – 'Charlie's in the wire!' (the warning of such incursions by Viet Cong last heard during the Vietnam war) – which fortunately proved false.

Although even in camp you were not necessarily safe, clearly travelling about was always a somewhat risky venture. I think my most nervous trip was on 11 September when I had to go down into the capital for a meeting,[12] thinking to myself, this place, the US embassy, Kabul, on this date, the tenth anniversary of 9/11 could well be about as dangerous a place to be as anywhere in the world.

However, I took the view that I was very much better paid than all those poor guys, particularly in the British and American RCs, who were in contact with the enemy and risking their necks on a daily basis. I had not been sent here in uniform to sit out my six months on the operation behind the wire, drawing my pay and consuming rations while delegating or expecting others to take all the risks, and apart from anything else I would have found it seriously boring. There was nothing heroic about this; it was a view taken by most of my comrades both in the legal office and beyond, although I was surprised to find that it was certainly not shared by all and there were people, including officers, to their shame, who would find every excuse in the book to avoid leaving the premises.

Although we felt we were some way behind the 'front line' of the forward operating bases (FOBs[13]) and the patrols out in the sticks, there were regular reminders that like most modern conflicts the ISAF battle space was not neatly delineated by perilous opposing firing lines backed up by a secure and stable hinterland of supporting infrastructure. Back in my Northern Ireland days I was always extremely thankful that our terrorist enemies of the Provisional Irish Republican Army (PIRA) and even the more vicious Irish National Liberation Army (INLA) never resorted to suicide tactics, but here in Afghanistan we enjoyed no such luxury.

Some areas of the country were serious hotspots for years on end, Helmand province being perhaps the most notorious, but equally there were none where safety and normality could be taken for granted by anybody. Just during my first few weeks in theatre two foolhardy German civilian climbers in their 60s who should have known better, walking in the apparently conflict-free area of the Salang Pass, went missing, their mutilated bodies predictably found a few days later, and a US Navy attached civilian wandered out of camp somewhere near Kabul, and very shortly met the same fate.

Closer to home, it had only been in April, a couple of months before I arrived, that an Afghan military pilot had opened fire and killed eight US Air Force personnel at a meeting in an office at the airport, and similar treacherous deliberate blue-on-blue incidents occurred in the coming weeks, an extremely frightening development which was almost impossible to guard against.

The insecurity was ever present, and even on my first day the headquarters was warned by that uselessly inaudible Tannoy system of an imminent rocket attack. This was a regular inconvenience, requiring helmets, body armour and loaded pistols[14] (although I never quite understood how that might help against rockets), and hours spent sheltering in the moderately 'hardened' accommodation blocks. At other times the alert state would be raised by other threats such as an impending suicide attack using a fuel tanker rammed through security gates or Taliban infiltration of the headquarters disguised as civilian contractors with forged ID cards.

The enforced daily close proximity in our little legal hut under this moderate but constant threat very rapidly generated an informal esprit de corps and an intimate knowledge of each other's anxieties, hopes and dreams which is probably unique to soldiers on duty a long way from home. The resemblance to 1950s *M.A.S.H.* did not entirely stop with the office infrastructure, as I rapidly found the American approach to their circumstances was in reality exactly the combination of laconic breeziness and dedication to duty portrayed by that fictional work.

Having sorted out taskings between Walt and me, we also managed to rusticate some of the captains, two of them on shifts out in the JOC, undoubtedly the most interesting place for them, and one to answer directly to an extremely demanding US brigadier-general. This brought welcome relief to the congestion in the 'Swamp' as we settled into our battle rhythm.

Apart from the usual morning fixture of the commander's 'stand up', there were a number of other regular events punctuating the working week. These included attendance at targeting boards, visits downtown to deal with compensation claims, one-star supervisory visits to report back on our progress and plans, twice-weekly internal office update meetings and Walt's loud and lengthy teleconferences with outlying JAG officers in their rule of law posts.

Saturday evening saw our regular social, a takeaway pizza, which was invariably excellent, then movie night which was equally reliably dire. Chief Ferrell boasted among his treasures an enormous trunk full of DVDs, many of which had been obtained at the bazaar for pennies. Their illicit provenance was given away in many cases by the sudden appearance in the film of random individuals apparently walking across the set, which is inevitably what you get when your production system simply involves smuggling a video recorder into the back of a cinema.

Irrespective of such technical deficiencies, I rapidly found the American soldier's taste in films and mine were rarely the same. Over the weeks we had such turkeys as *Captain America*, which they adored, *Spaceballs*, which was just that, *Transformers*, which was unspeakable, *Planet of the Apes* and *The Big Lebowski*. I just didn't get it, especially as Walt prided himself on being an English literature graduate, but not wanting to seem like the snotty Brit I would politely attend, and keep my thoughts to myself, usually sneaking out quietly after a few minutes.

Most postal deliveries to the office seemed to include an influx of goodies, from a dozen large pecan pies for Katy on her birthday – 'The best birthday I have ever had – in Afghanistan' – to half a smoked salmon, to what seemed to be the entire buffet from a party held by Andy's family in his support. My colleagues were very generous and just loved their snacks, with office business constantly accompanied by a background of comparing notes on the latest treats, and contented chewing and crunching, like feeding time in the primate house at the zoo.

The variety of work coming through the door supplementing our core business kept life colourful, not least when trying to resolve the matter of so many different jurisdictions which might apply. A lot of time was spent refining the no alcohol rule, because although the HQ was US commanded, it was legally every bit as much an international construct as HQ KFOR had been all those years ago. Thus, a number of countries wanted the rule relaxed to permit exceptions on national days, but with so many nations represented this would have meant some sort of party practically every week of the year so in the end it was simpler for all to fall in line with the total ban of General Order No. 1.

Not all soldiers agreed, one example being a quiet get-together over a bottle of vodka between a British lance-corporal, a young Belgian soldier and a female US army driver. All would have been well had the driver not been stopped at the wheel by one of the garrison military police and found to be clearly the worse for wear. Each was reported to their respective chain of command for national investigation, because neither NATO or ISAF have any military legal system of their own. Their different nations' reactions were interesting. The US driver was fined and sent home, the Brit's case was advised on by the legal office down at the UK Joint Force Support establishment at Camp Bastion in Helmand (manned by a couple of my UK ALS colleagues), and eventually also fined. The Belgian just went back to work, after a mild informal rebuke.

On another occasion we found ourselves dealing with a personnel issue involving a US female lieutenant working under two Brits and another American, who was so surly and useless at her job that they initiated a removal from post. As soon as she got wind of this but before any formal steps had been taken, she cunningly initiated a harassment complaint against all three. This instantly put a stop to any prospect of moving her, pending resolution, and caused two different national harassment response processes to kick in, initially both advised in the one legal office, ours, and put the three officers complained against, who still commanded the complainant, on the defensive.

The US inclination, understandably, was to remove the complainant from theatre, which of course she didn't want, and they were stuck with her. Such relatively small beer could have caused real problems in a tight-knit multinational workplace like this. Eventually 'work arounds' were devised but the staff effort involved in such cases was an unwelcome distraction from our mission.

Such jurisdictional shenanigans also applied in more serious matters, such as 'the great generator heist' in which a number of arrests were made by the International Military Police on camp. CCTV footage had

Welcome to Kabul

disclosed two low loaders driven by Afghan civilians blagging their way into camp and making off into the night a couple of hours later with three generators, worth about $50,000 each, lifted from a building project. This was by far the most exciting thing that had happened on the ChIMP's watch, after many boring months in theatre and he was determined to make the most of it.

Suspect number one was a British civilian who worked for a British private security company, of which inevitably there were many operating in Kabul. Some were subject to British jurisdiction for criminal matters, but only those which were registered under the applicable Military Technical Agreement (the reader will remember all about MTAs from Kosovo). Unfortunately for this chap his employers were not so registered, meaning that he was simply subject to Afghan criminal jurisdiction. He was detained for a couple of days in a cell at the airport which would no doubt have horrified Human Rights Watch, and interrogated personally by ChIMP, who threatened to turn him over to the Afghans. At that point the initially tight-lipped suspect very sensibly decided it would be a good idea to come clean. He admitted being paid $20,000 for his part in the caper and implicated a fellow Brit, who was the KAIA DFAC manager, working for an MTA-registered company, Kellogg Brown and Root (KBR[15]) and a US civilian, as his two accomplices.

In the end it seemed that the Afghans were not interested in pursuing suspect number one, luckily for him, and he was pragmatically deprived of his $20,000 and put on the first plane home. However, the US, although unable to devise any jurisdiction over suspect number one, very much got their teeth into the other two. In order to plug a lacuna in their jurisdiction over US civilians accompanying the military overseas Congress had passed the Military Extra Territorial Jurisdiction Act (MEJA) 2000 enabling them to prosecute anybody 'employed by or accompanying the armed forces overseas' for offences carrying twelve months' imprisonment or more. What's more, it was not only applicable to suspect number two, the American in this case, but arguably also to the KBR man because of KBR's contractual connection with the US.

I had to admire the proactive approach of the US embassy legal office, who had restraining orders issued for these two, preventing them leaving the country before the ink was dry on the ChIMP's report. At the time I thought it was rather cheeky to be assuming jurisdiction over the Brit, who was concurrently subject to UK jurisdiction under the MTA, without even consulting me first, and I told them so. Either British or US jurisdiction would have entailed a court martial, which was eventually deemed inappropriate for the KBR manager who was probably the smaller cog of the three, so he too was summarily sent home at his own expense. However, the US civilian was dragged kicking and screaming back to the States to an uncertain fate. The Afghan drivers disappeared without trace, as did the generators.

With all this variety of work and the different landmarks in the weekly calendar, each day's routine was slightly different. It also helped that although most of our lives were spent behind the wire there were constant comings and goings and people-watching opportunities.

The most unexpected of these was 'Legends of Aerospace', three of whom turned up one day as part of a tour laid on by the US Morale and Welfare organization. It wasn't exactly Vera Lynn but nor is it every day you get to see Neil Armstrong, who died less than a year later. Our famous visitors were greeted with lots of whooping and cheering by their compatriots, calling them 'our heroes', to which they graciously replied that 'today you are ours'.

Less glamorous but equally exotic in their own way were our transient special forces soldiers, or Special Ops Forces (SOF) as the US calls them. As I noted in my diary at the time:

> If you are SOF it is mandatory to demonstrate your machismo and disdain for military norms by sporting a beard, although the instinct for uniformity seems to demand all such beards must be of the same impressive dimensions (shades of the Taliban insistence on one fist's width from the chin). You should also stand about in the gym for long periods whilst pretending unsuccessfully not to look in the mirror, in between grunting over ridiculous weights. If in uniform, never ever wear a hat (displaying carefully dishevelled hair), or badges of rank, or other insignia (apart from the mandatory daggers tattooed on the forearms). Studiously ignore others you pass on the street (no eye contact or greeting) and be seen as often as possible alighting from an armoured 4x4, bedecked with weaponry around the waist, before removing a sniper rifle from the boot, or sometimes a sinister-looking case presumably containing a dismantled

weapon of some description. When eating (gargantuan helpings), you should either be alone, or with no more than one other person (male, who must also have a beard) but even then, only speak to request a napkin.

By way of a complete contrast to that, one morning at breakfast I observed a rather touching scenario of old-fashioned manners which struck me as uniquely American. I had noticed how cheerful and polite the black American soldiers invariably seemed and on this occasion three of them sat down opposite me and held hands while they said grace before starting their meal. At that point another, queuing for his food, called across to them to say he'd join them and they all stopped eating to wait for him. Then once he had sat down, they all four held hands and repeated their grace before starting again.

Other birds of a completely different feather who were encountered in some numbers around camp were the civilian contractors and 'analysts'. These were largely ex-US servicemen and came in all shapes and sizes, but were almost always both very hairy and very overweight. They had swapped one uniform for another in civvy street: baseball caps, T-shirts and khaki cargo pants and Caterpillar boots, with heavy-duty pistols strapped to even heavier-duty thighs.

These characters tended to fall into two principal categories. There were the sad ones from broken relationships back home who were happy to spend eighteen months at a time in chaotic failed states picking up tax-free pay packets for attending endless meetings and sending endless emails. These overlapped with the professional drifters who were hired for three months at a time with lucrative contracts from some UN agency, NATO or Uncle Sam to bring their expertise on mineral extraction in the DR Congo or HIV in Mexico[16] to Afghanistan.

Much of the work of this high-priced army, ancillary to ISAF, was to gather the 'metrics' needed to feed the strategic military and political beasts so that governments could go on persuading themselves that progress was being made in return for their open-ended expenditure of blood and treasure.

Almost a decade had already elapsed since the Taliban were removed from office, in just the latest in at least 200 years of failed attempts by outsiders to bring this unruly country to heel. Official optimism was inevitably matched by the more sceptical view that 'while we have the

Rolexes the insurgents have the time', and although Tinkerbell was kept alive by all the children willing it so, there was precious little hard evidence of the desired effect here.

It wasn't as if we were on Devil's Island or an Antarctic research station but some people did seem to go a bit wire happy if they spent too long on this mission. During the summer a vain attempt had been made to create a green refuge, complete with roses and gazebos, out of the unpromising dust in the middle of camp, a little pretentiously named 'The Aryana Gardens'. One very cold November evening, walking briskly back to my quarters in the dark, I came across a group of half a dozen US officers, looking rather self-conscious, gathered in one of these gazebos talking loudly and puffing on enormous Havanas. Nobody had even bothered with this would-be garden during warm summer evenings, so why now, maybe a birthday?

Then round the next block, squatting uncomfortably in the gloom right up against the perimeter wire was a US female soldier plucking disconsolately at a guitar.

I looked up for a full moon, but no, it wasn't that.

Chapter 7

Kill or Capture

The law of war, which in recent years has been redefined as the law of armed conflict, has long been very clear[1] that civilians caught up in it should not be harmed, let alone killed. Unfortunately, just as the law has become better developed and disseminated since the mid-nineteenth century, its ability to protect civilians has been fatally undermined by coincidental developments in military technology and the very nature of armed conflict. Statistical comparisons between numbers of civilians versus soldiers killed during major armed conflicts across the globe during the past century, beginning with the First World War, make for depressing reading.[2]

Having said that, there is some good news, in that even in the most unlikely theatres of operations politicians are seemingly getting the message that accountability on the world stage and legitimacy in their methods matter more and more in today's global village. For example, during my time at the MoD, I visited Bogota on a number of occasions to help the Colombian armed forces develop ROE in their fifty-year struggle against the FARC.[3] For much of that time the counterinsurgency campaign had been severely undermined by allegations of brutality, extra-judicial killings and other human rights abuses by government forces.

The most rewarding event during my modest venture to provide some legal input in that US backyard was a meeting with the then Colombian defence minister Juan Manuel Santos. He made it very clear that he believed that strict adherence to LOAC was paramount for the legitimacy of the government's campaign, irrespective of the behaviour of the adversary. A few years later he went on to become President Santos, the man who brought peace to his country after a very dark and bitter age by achieving reconciliation with the FARC, for which he was awarded the Nobel Peace Prize in 2016.

As any lawyer knows, jurisdiction is everything; to try and advise a client without determining the jurisdiction governing the client's legal problem is to try to fight with at least one arm tied behind your back, and at the risk of being boringly repetitive, jurisdiction can hinge upon many different factors. We have already seen how that jurisdictional issue caused problems in Kosovo and how it had to be resolved in Kabul, even when dealing with legal problems peripheral to the conduct of the military operation.

When out fighting on the ground in Afghanistan, every ISAF nation was bound by the jurisdiction of customary international law and the various treaties, in particular Geneva law, to which they were parties. At the same time, like the Colombians dealing with the FARC, ISAF faced an adversary which, although they did operate under their own code (in this case a combination of *Pashtunwali* and Islam), it had nothing whatever to do with Geneva law and any adherence by them to customary law was purely coincidental.

This conflict started off in 2001 as an international armed conflict (IAC) between the Afghan government (at that time the Taliban) forces and those of the US and her allies, but after the Taliban had been ousted and replaced by the Karzai government, the legal classification of the conflict changed. It had now become a non-international armed conflict (NIAC) between the now insurgent Taliban irregulars and various associated networks like the Haqqanis on the one hand, and the Afghan government's national armed forces with their ISAF allies on the other.

What doesn't help in Afghanistan is the very warlike and bloodthirsty temperament of many of its people, which the British learnt to their cost many years ago. Indeed in 1890, in the final verse of his poem 'The Young British Soldier', Kipling wrote:

> *When you're wounded and left on Afghanistan's plains,*
> *And the women come out to cut up what remains,*
> *Jest roll to your rifle and blow out your brains*
> *An' go to your Gawd like a soldier ...*
> *So-oldier of the Queen!*

Over a century later the young British soldiers of another queen found themselves fighting the same enemy. The principal hostile elements of the Taliban are drawn from the Pashtun tribe, hence 'Pashtunwali', known in Kipling's day as Pathans, ferocious fighters who were always best kept onside, but historically seldom have been. In fact, they hate the British even more than the Americans, because despite repeated defeats we seem to keep returning to their country for more.

It is said that when word of a British or US patrol approaching a rural village in Iraq reached its people, the men would hide in their houses and the women would rush outside to round up their children before joining them, and there they all would sit tight until hopefully the danger moved on. In contrast, in Afghanistan the women would hide in the house with their babies and daughters but every male inhabitant who was strong enough to hold a weapon (often ancient) would take up a firing position and open up with everything they'd got the moment the patrol came within range,[4] if not before.

Whether in countries with such a reputation or in more peaceful parts of the world, governments tend to be very reluctant to admit that internal violence has reached a stage which amounts to NIAC. This is for a number of reasons, perhaps the two most important being these.

First, such an admission tells the rest of the world that this government has been so ineffective that it cannot control its own people within its own borders. Secondly, once a NIAC has broken out, international law partly usurps domestic law (good old 'jurisdiction' again); in other words, the government has lost control legally as well as practically. Just to complicate matters further, the classification of an insurgency as either amounting to a NIAC or not depends on such issues as the level of violence involved, or who actually holds the ground, which can vary from time to time and from one part of the country to another.

In parts of Colombia the FARC were so dominant that they, and not the government's forces, were in control, so in those regions the violence amounted to a NIAC, while in the neighbouring province all was fairly quiet so there was no NIAC and no LOAC involvement. The maximum legitimate level of violence which any government forces could employ in those relatively peaceful areas, where only domestic law applied, would be for self-defence[5] (like the British army during the Northern Ireland 'Troubles'). But in Colombia that might change on the next day, and then indeed change back again. No wonder they had trouble keeping up, and kept running into legitimacy arguments.

The situation was not dissimilar in Afghanistan, with the level of violence and Taliban influence varying considerably across the country and the Karzai government undecided whether or not to admit that they had a NIAC on their hands. This caused me great difficulty in one of my tasks, to try and devise a set of ROE for the ANA and train them how to apply them. By the time I had arrived and attempted that job, the conflict had already been ongoing for nearly a decade and I don't believe it has even been achieved as I write, another decade later.

This problem of the 'classification of conflict' was neatly summarized by US Marine Corps General Charles Krulak in the late 1990s. He talked about the 'three block war', in which a soldier could find himself fighting under three differing legal jurisdictions as he moved from one city block to the next, and the next, depending on the level of violence he was dealing with. The notion led to another term, the 'strategic corporal' – the guy whose split-second decision-making on how to react to that violence, captured on CNN and seen around the world within a matter of hours, could thereby have a strategic effect on the whole operation, especially if he got it wrong, despite his modest rank.

Looking back at the beginning of this chapter, what does this all have to do with civilians, and why is it important? The answer is that in a NIAC the legal status of soldiers of the government and their allies, in this case ISAF, means that they are permitted to fight. The presumed legal status of the Afghan population is the same as in an IAC; they are civilians, neither permitted to fight nor legitimate targets, and entitled to protection from attack. The big 'but' is that once a civilian does directly participate,[6] he loses his civilian status and all the legal protection from attack which goes with it and he may be killed or captured, with no obligation on his adversary to try to capture him instead of killing him.[7]

Prisoners of war must legally be released upon the cessation of hostilities, but civilians captured whilst directly participating in hostilities in a NIAC are not prisoners of war. They are good, ordinary criminals, liable to be handed over to the national police and thereafter prosecuted for whatever crimes they may have committed under national law. On conviction for, say, murder they are liable to whatever penalty their national law provides, which may of course include a prison sentence continuing long after the fighting has ended, or indeed even capital punishment.

So far, so straightforward – if only. The problem is, how to define 'direct participation in hostilities' (DPH), literally a matter of life or death in somewhere like Afghanistan, home of the 'Ten dollar Taliban'.[8] Inevitably, this has become one of the most fruitful subjects for controversy amongst lawyers, academics, soldiers and politicians in the whole field of LOAC.[9]

The two extremes of the definition of somebody who is DPH go something like this. The most cautious approach is to maintain that this is a conduct-based definition and only applicable at the time the suspect is actually doing something which amounts to direct participation, committing a hostile act such as firing on the adversary. Arising from this is the 'revolving door' debate, farmer by day, fighter by night. Thus, when the farmer gets up in the early hours to walk a mile to plant an IED in the road, few would dispute that while he's planting it at 5 am, he is DPH, but some say that when he got up at 4 am to set off and when he got back to his house for breakfast at 6 am, he was not directly participating. But when did DPH start, 4.30 am? and when did it finish, 5.30 am? Does it make a difference if he only does this once a week, or once a month, or just once?

I'm reminded of this by the *Dad's Army* theme tune: 'Mr Brown goes off to town on the 8.21, but he comes home each evening and he's ready with his gun.' The Home Guard's legal status in the UK during the Second World War was probably clear enough, but these lines neatly sum up the 'revolving door' issue.

At the other end of the scale there is an equally strongly held view that the DPH definition stretches all the way from the above to including mere status, such as membership of an armed group (MOAG), even if the suspect himself is not actually fighting, never has and never intends to, such as a 'mere' fundraiser for the campaign. In fact, the whole issue of funding for the insurgency, made particularly unfathomable by the locals' use of the *hawala*[10] secret banking system, added to the complexity of an already 'wicked' problem.

Some argue, however, that membership of such groups is not sufficient per se, and they must have a 'continuous combat function' within that group to be DPH. After all, even in regular uniformed government armed forces some personnel such as medics enjoy certain protections. If there is such a thing as a Taliban medic, shouldn't he enjoy equivalent protected status?

ISAF's interpretation of the law was somewhere in the middle. Those committing a 'hostile act', or demonstrating 'hostile intent'[11] were clearly lawful targets, as were MOAG such as the Taliban or the Haqqani network. However, targeting rules for identifying people wherever they were to be found in the spectrum were extremely strict, requiring a well proven and very direct nexus between fundraising and fighting, for example, which was pretty impossible to establish.

All this is great material for lawyers, but what about soldiers in the field, on the receiving end of that IED?

Not everyone was happy with what they saw as wishy-washy restraint on effective measures to combat ISAF's enemies. I once found myself in a meeting chaired by a US colonel steaming with fury that whenever his unit captured Taliban financiers and handed them over to the Afghans as required, they were released within days, after an appropriate sum had changed hands. His proposed solution was to have them added in the first place to the target list,[12] with or without clearing the high evidence threshold which ISAF demanded.

The meeting ended rather ungraciously, with the understandably frustrated colonel beginning to sound as if he'd been watching too many movies. He described one prisoner who was probably highly suspect and dangerous, but was nevertheless not a lawful ISAF target, as looking 'real good in orange', à la Guantanamo Bay, and muttering darkly that if ISAF wouldn't 'do it' (whatever 'it' was), the 'US has its own means'. I couldn't help thinking of the bad old days in Northern Ireland, when the British government became extremely frustrated at US inaction over blatant fundraising in the States for the PIRA by NORAID, although I decided it might be a little provocative to remind our fuming friend.

ISAF's identification of those directly participating in hostilities involved intelligence gathering all over the country, employing a variety of means to produce a matrix of suspects' names. If you were unlucky enough to be amongst those names your likelihood of becoming an approved target depended where you stood on the vertical alphabetic scale of the reliability of the intelligence and the horizontal numerical scale of its credibility. Each regional command submitted its updated matrix once a week to IJC for approval by a two-star chaired 'Targeting Board'. At any one time the theatre-wide target list would number several hundred.

Contrary to some sceptical assumptions, target approval was no rubber-stamping exercise and each name was continuously reviewed, with the individual's 'pattern of life' and identity examined minutely. The addition of names to the target list, from which they automatically timed out after a fixed period unless reconfirmed, was only the first stage of the process. To avoid mistakes, nobody was to be deliberately targeted unless positively identified (PID) as the individual named on the approved target list.

The Taliban were formidable opponents, not only for their fighters' renowned courage and physical resilience but also their cunning and ruthlessness. In the early days they sometimes made relatively easy targets because they could not resist using mobile phones, until they understood that this was like erecting a large sign saying 'I am the target' and bringing down Hellfire missile attacks out of nowhere. Taliban commanders then took to sabotaging rebro' masts before an attack, so that even inadvertent breaches of 'radio silence' became impossible. They would change names, which were already confusing enough to the westerner, flit backwards and forwards across into the untouchable haven of Pakistan at will,[13] and were quite happy to wire up innocent or naïve disciples of any age or gender[14] with suicide vests and send them to their deaths.

Identical techniques were employed by the Taliban's brothers in arms, the Haqqani network, who, for example, famously assassinated Afghanistan's former president, Burhanuddin Rabbani on 20 September 2011 at his house inside the Green Zone by sending in a fighter, on the pretext of negotiations, with a bomb hidden in his turban.

ISAF in turn gradually learned to respect their enemies' lethal ability to exploit its mistakes, not least on those inevitable occasions when innocent civilians were killed.

In recognition of the 'fog of war', LOAC allows a margin of error in military operations so that some collateral death or destruction can happen without the perpetrator facing prosecution.[15] However, the law also imposes on soldiers a requirement to take stringent precautions in attack to minimize collateral risk.[16] The better equipped and therefore more lethal you are, and the more senior you are, the heavier the precautionary burden. As we have seen from Kosovo days, some of the most important tools for implementing this requirement are ROE, and in ISAF it was also the full-time job of the targeting boards and the Target Operations Cell (TOC) to make sure we got it right.

Working with the US Army I learnt very quickly that their whole ethos was extremely 'forward leaning', which is their equivalent, I suppose, of the 'can do attitude', also encouraged in the British forces. My JAG colleagues tended to reflect this approach by saying they believed in being 'green light' lawyers, another way of saying that, like any good lawyer they believed in finding a way for their client to get what he or she wanted.

However, the danger of defaulting to the 'green light' preference, particularly for the less experienced lawyer advising very senior officers, is of being overawed by that differential in rank and experience and being too eager always to oblige. Civilian clients may be extremely valuable to your firm's business but they tend not to be wearing your uniform, with rank badges often indicating that they are considerably senior to you in a chain of command which directly plots the course of your career. Furthermore, with the exception of those employed as *consiglieri* to mafia bosses, civilian lawyers tend not to be called upon to give literally 'life or death' advice.

Eager commanders would usually phrase their request for advice as 'Can I?' or 'Could I?' do whatever it was they wanted to do, e.g. strike a particular target. We learnt that it was often important, even when the answer was strictly speaking 'Yes you could' to add the supplementary question 'Should I?' This might sound more like operational advice than legal advice but the danger was that if we just stopped at the 'Yes you could' answer, no further thought was given to the proposal before taking the action, and then if it all went horribly wrong the lawyers could be blamed because they had said it was legally OK. To put it crudely, it's a good way to cover both commander's and lawyer's arses. I was often reminded of this when asked for advice and I always thought if you must refer to traffic lights when advising on matters such as targeting, amber is a better colour.

A US unit near Kabul wanted legal support for the idea of using paintball guns to deter annoying kids from coming up to their perimeter fence to try and steal things and generally have fun winding them up. The toy guns were kept in stock amongst US 'Morale and Welfare' equipment and I must say I found it a bit odd, if not worrying, that soldiers might want to unwind during their time off duty from armed patrolling by fighting one another with paintball guns, but each to his own.

I imagined it ending badly, with the world's media showing what the mighty US had sunk to, children's faces running with red paint claimed to be blood, or a child blinded by an unlucky shot in the head (quite apart from the fact that once they had cottoned on, the kids would have loved it and just tried harder for the reaction). It was easy enough for ISAF to fall foul of the international court of public opinion without asking for trouble unnecessarily and my advice was, yes you could do it but I strongly suggest you don't; they didn't.

One evening another unit submitted a targeting request on two men seen carrying bags over their shoulders out into a known IED 'minefield', apparently digging up devices and carrying them away for use elsewhere – hostile act – may we open fire? It was getting dark and the UAV proposed for the strike was running out of loiter time. We approved, but only subject to clarification by the aircraft's camera first. Just as well – they turned out to be boys digging up onions. It was so easy to get these things wrong.

On another potentially much more serious occasion one ISAF nation, always keen to exploit their tremendous technical resources, came up with a detonation system designed to be flown along routes known to be regularly 'seeded' with IEDs which would set them all off from the air, a bit like a modern airborne equivalent of a D-Day flail tank. The problem was that it would be impossible to prevent such a system taking out innocent passers-by who happened to be on the route when the devices were being remotely detonated. In many ways it was a brilliant idea, but the legal view that this breached the precautionary principle prevailed.

Hellfire missiles were extremely effective at destroying vehicles but it was not unusual for their occupants still to be seen debussing and crawling, limping, hopping, or even legging it at high speed for cover. The question then was, 'Can we go around and have another shot at them?' The answer sounds like 'Of course you can, assuming they have been positively identified as a legitimate target', but it's not as simple as that. You need to know if they appear to be wounded, and if so, how badly. The LOAC rule of *hors de combat* ('out of the fight') says that where somebody is so badly injured as to be incapable of effectively continuing to fight, he is no longer a lawful target.[17]

When things did go wrong, sometimes even on a fairly minor scale, all hell tended to break loose. This was partly because of the dubious stability of President Mohamed Karzai. He was a complex character, allegedly himself rather too fond of some of his country's unusual agricultural products, and must have been a nightmare for ISAF commanders and diplomats to handle at times. On numerous occasions Karzai threatened to expel ISAF following actions in which – supposedly, because they certainly weren't always – innocent bystanders had been killed or maimed. No doubt the president was genuinely concerned about innocent casualties amongst his subjects but there was also often an element of self-serving grandstanding in his reaction. After all, he was a man who had good reason to fear the Taliban himself, but in any event the spin-off from his outbursts in the international community was a serious strategic problem.

The reaction – some said overreaction – of ISAF commanders was severe. 'Tactical directives' were issued and among other things it was decreed that, no matter what the law actually allowed, there were in future to be zero collateral deaths.[18] One legal pitfall of such a restriction lies in customary international law because as we have already seen, the law develops largely through 'state practice', so if you keep doing something you might find it has actually crept up on you to become a limitation by which you have become legally bound, instead of a discretionary temporary measure.

General McChrystal's order was for ISAF to exercise 'courageous restraint' but putting it into practice was easier said than done. His successor, General Petraeus, tried again, with the equally worthy 'tactical patience'. These slogans were no doubt carefully considered, but such perceived limitations on their freedom of action were confusing and far from popular with most soldiers.

Mistakes still happened, usually minor but sometimes extremely serious. On one occasion, in the Kunduz area, within Regional Command North, the Taliban managed to hijack two fuel tankers coming in from Tajikistan and bound for ISAF. Things went from bad to worse, as one of them got stuck trying to cross a river, at which point word rapidly spread locally that there was precious fuel there for the taking by anybody in the area. Scores of men, women and children appeared from nowhere, armed with any bucket or jerrycan they could lay their hands on.

Believing all this to be an insurgent operation, the German chain of command called in a US airstrike. An airstrike on a laden fuel tanker can only end one way, and, sure enough, dozens of people were horrifically maimed, with estimates for the dead ranging from sixty to one hundred and fifty. Although none of them were up to any good, it rapidly became clear that most of the casualties, far from having even the remotest connection with the insurgency, were no more than petty opportunists. The ISAF operation yet again survived the outrage, but not without political heads rolling in Germany.[19]

On another occasion during my time an equally serious own goal occurred, this time with Pakistan on the receiving end. Like a long-standing unsatisfactory marriage, ISAF and Pakistan reluctantly needed each other. Pakistan received substantial aid from the US and reaped a further fortune for permitting our logistic supply route from the port of Karachi up to landlocked Afghanistan, and ISAF in turn was heavily dependent on Pakistan both for that physical lifeline and for at least some degree of cooperation from their military.

However, relations between ISAF, but particularly the US, and Pakistan were chronically fragile, having worsened considerably earlier in 2011 with the infringement of Pakistan's sovereignty during the Bin Laden sting operation in Abbottabad. Afghanistan deeply mistrusted and resented Pakistan for the blind eye which was blatantly turned to Taliban activities conducted with impunity on their soil, from where it was well known that the Taliban high command actually directed operations against ISAF.[20] Intelligence also indicated that the vast majority of the agrochemicals used for the Taliban's explosives came from two factories just inside Pakistan, but since even cross-border hot pursuits were forbidden, nothing could be done about either problem without Pakistan's assistance.

In the context of this uneasy relationship, upsetting Pakistan could have strategic consequences every bit as severe as upsetting President Karzai, and boy, did we upset them one night in November 2011.

By almost unbelievable coincidence, it was literally as COMISAF was travelling back from a meeting in Pakistan with their army chief of staff that a US Apache helicopter took out a Pakistani border post on the Khyber Pass, killing twenty-eight of their soldiers. Of course, this was a matter of mistaken identity and there was a lot of argument at that time suggesting they had been straying over the border into Afghanistan (probably true although hotly denied by Pakistan), giving rise to an understandable belief that they were Afghan insurgents.

NATO issued profuse public apologies, although the German public information brigadier responsible looked very uncomfortable on TV doing so. This was probably because there was a strong rumour that it was actually a US national 'Op Enduring Freedom' asset which had done the deed and nothing to do with ISAF and they were just 'taking it on the chin' to spare US blushes. Then an Afghan police general also waded into the debate, saying it was the best thing the US had done in ten years because Pakistan did nothing but cause ISAF trouble, which didn't help much to calm things down.

Finally, we were advised that a so-called 'tiger team' – whatever one of those is – would be investigating. Pakistan was unimpressed, closing the border crossings at Torkham Gate and Weesh Shaman, which effectively blockaded the road up from Karachi, and withdrawing from the unfortunately timed imminent Bonn diplomatic conference, convened to review ISAF's progress.

Walt was doing a great job energizing all his JAG colleagues out in the field with their thankless rule of law tasks, hard enough to sell there as a concept[21] but made all the more impossible by the limited life expectancy of judges and prosecutors. I had decided early on that quite apart from my personal aversion to going stir crazy, it was important that my contribution to the campaign should also include more than just sitting in the office.

The opportunity to escape came from my friends in the Targeting Operations Cell, who were setting up a series of road trips to the regional commands to brief a selection of groups, including their opposite numbers in the field, on current practice and procedure. ROE were an important element of this business and I was invited along to field any legal aspects.

The first trip, in mid-September, by which time temperatures in the lowlands were becoming more bearable, was to HQ RC West at Herat, near the Iranian border, home to about 3,000 Italian troops which they shared with a Spanish unit, the inevitable US and even a small Albanian contingent.

Like most military hops around the country our transport was a C-130 Hercules, a workhorse of an aircraft which is not really designed for passengers, with 'seats' like canvas camp chairs slung along the sides of the fuselage, facing in, so sightseeing out of the little portholes invariably comes at the cost of a stiff neck. Nevertheless, having seen precious little of this mysterious country so far, I was looking forward to the trip and spent the two-hour flight in cloudless skies peering out at an awkward angle.

Not so long ago much of Afghanistan was either green or forested but the combination of climate change and human exploitation has changed all that. Certainly, what I could see of this western half of the country appeared to consist largely of either mountainous dust or flat dust. Very occasionally one could see a village, comprising walled compounds (made of dust, of course), linked to the next by unmetalled (dust) tracks, but over what must have been more than 300 miles I barely saw any signs of irrigation or cultivation. Perhaps this is where the expression 'dirt poor' originates – it certainly never seemed more appropriate.

Nevertheless, approaching our destination, the country was glowingly beautiful in the late evening sunlight and we had a tantalizing glimpse of the minarets and domes of Herat, one of the most picturesque and historic cities in the country and a Silk Road landmark, unfortunately not amenable to military tourism despite being relatively calm. The base, also covered in dust, was a little like IJC on a smaller scale, being co-located with the airport at the edge of town, but as we stepped out of the aircraft the air was noticeably cleaner than in Kabul, and it felt refreshingly rural.

We were met by an Italian Air Force colonel and shown to our quarters by his Puglian warrant officer, Vito, before reconvening for dinner. This was preceded by a luxury unknown at KAIA, a cold beer, true amber nectar after a couple of months' abstinence. Dinner was also an Italian treat, complete with grissini and antipasto and washed down with a very welcome bottle of rosso.

The next day we presented our pitch, the targeting business being very well received, despite language and technical complexities. Later, I was able to dig out the Italian captain who posed as their legal officer, who had an irritating inability to reply to emails. He was very polite, and rather unconvincingly pleaded overwork and language difficulties. Fortunately, he was just about to finish his minimalist three months' deployment, apparently with two replacements, so hopefully things would improve and at least I now had other contacts there. RC West was operationally something of a sleepy backwater and I had my doubts about how much of our targeting wisdom was ever likely to be put into practice but it had still been very useful for both hosts and visitors to 'press the flesh'.

All air forces seem to share the RAF's malicious pleasure in demanding ridiculous check in margins, so we were up at 4.30 the following morning for our (delayed) 7 am flight back to Kabul but the fresh desert morning air, spectacular sunrise and just the experience of being out and about more than compensated.

About a week later I found myself up at the same hour, this time for the trip up north to Mazar i Sharif, HQ RC North, which was run by the Germans but also manned by some US personnel and a number of Scandinavian units. Here it was 'smokin' hot', to use one of Walt's favourite terms, but the contrast with Herat in other respects was as Nuremberg is to Naples. We were met by a smart Mercedes G Wagen and driven on an immaculate concrete perimeter road which was literally being swept of desert dust by uniformed workmen, to accommodation as solid and tidy as only to be expected from the Bundeswehr. Everywhere was meticulously signposted, vehicles neatly parked in rows and most buildings equipped with aircon and flat-screen TVs.

The following day we conducted our briefing before an extremely attentive audience who kept us on our toes with a barrage of largely sensible questions. Afterwards I met the German legal adviser, senior and rather more serious minded than his Herat counterpart, and then went off with my targeting colleagues to have a look at a UAV.

These 'drones' came into their own on this operation. I remembered their early days when we were in Kosovo but the technology a decade later was so much advanced as to be unrecognizable. The more successful this remotely controlled weaponry was, the more legally and politically controversial, but even if it is flown by men halfway round the world in the Nevada desert, it relies on the same sort of input from that 'pilot' thousands of miles away as a jet fighter does with him sitting in the cockpit.

It can fly much more slowly and quietly than a fighter jet, so the likelihood of mistaken target identification such as we saw all too often in Kosovo using conventional aircraft is in fact reduced. Any complex new weapon system deserves critical appraisal[22] but often the problem is with the operator or the political direction rather than the technology. In this case the control room was in a container a matter of yards away from the aircraft itself, tucked away in a corner of its enormous hangar awaiting the next sortie, up to twenty-seven hours in the air.

As I discovered walking around later, this already enormous camp was still growing, with military hardware from Swedish MRAPs[23] to fuel tankers and APCs in all shapes and colours with the markings of half a dozen different nations. Whereas some had clearly seen their share of active duty, others were as shiny as the day they left the factory. Much had been shipped via Karachi but as much again would have come the long way round, overland from Western Europe via Russia and the 'Stans. I couldn't help wondering how it would all get back again, as one by one the ISAF contributing nations began to draw down taking their cue from the US who were due to reduce by at least 10,000 men by that very Christmas.

We dined, as you would expect, on Jägerschnitzel and, in accordance with a Teutonic version of General Order No. 1, non-alcoholic beer until 8 pm, after which a proper one was permitted, and during our meal we learnt a little more about life in this HQ.

A fighter pilot approaching the end of his tour recounted how some months ago, at the height of the summer the camp commander had been both perplexed and alarmed to discover that the HQ's water consumption had mysteriously shot up to an unprecedented level in a matter of weeks.

All attempts to trace where this lake of water had gone drew a complete blank until the commander was inspired to try aerial surveillance, and a jet returning from a combat mission was tasked to make a couple of circuits of camp with cameras running before landing.

Thus, our narrator informed us rather smugly, he solved the mystery with a couple of passes in his Tornado. The low-level digital footage recorded that no fewer than a dozen swimming pools had been constructed from adapted shipping containers, visible only from the air. As it then transpired, these had been hosting regular pool parties complete with scantily clad off-duty Scandinavian nymphettes enjoying a refreshing dip under the Afghan sun. Clearly '*das ist nicht normal-und streng verboten*'!

Our next trip, a few weeks later, was to Kandahar, Afghanistan's second city and heartland of the Taliban. This part of the country had seen a lot of activity right from the start, including, unusually, set-piece battles between ISAF and the Taliban. Canada had suffered particularly in the early days and had recently pulled out of the ISAF mission which had become extremely politically unpopular back home. Given the intensity of operations in the area, it was inevitably special forces heavy and we were there to brief a recently arrived SAS unit.

We flew in as usual by Hercules, although by this time I had given up my contortions to try and see the view, having concluded that at least from the air, the country looked very much the same everywhere. We landed on a chilly Saturday evening at yet another dusty airport on the edge of the camp. Somewhere in the middle of this enormous headquarters we were shown the usual basic accommodation and turned in early.

I was awoken at about 4 am by a distant thud which gently shook the building, followed by a long whistling sound, straight out of *Oh, What a Lovely War*,[24] which came closer and closer, and finally a very loud bang and rather more serious shaking. This was clearly a rocket attack (hard though it was to accept as the real thing with these Bugs Bunny sound effects), so I dutifully leapt out of bed and lay face down underneath it as per instructions, quivering slightly in anticipation of more incoming.

Nothing happened for a bit and it was very cold, so taking my life in my hands, I retrieved my duvet before re-adopting the position. Still nothing, except a distant vehicle siren, then the rocket alarm (a bit late!). I was contemplating trying to find the shelter, but remembering the slightly embarrassing night of the Skopje earthquake incident, I had already decided to stay put when the 'all clear' followed and I clambered gratefully back into bed.

At breakfast the next morning I was relieved to find that I had not just imagined the whole thing, as everybody else had been woken by it too. This was an almost nightly event in these parts, the culprits being cheap Chinese weapons with a range of about five miles, which were highly inaccurate but would of course ruin your day if you were unlucky enough to be on the receiving end. The Kandahar base housed thousands of people so even a poor-quality, inaccurate weapon like this could do a lot of damage, especially with so many aircraft parked in the open, but on this occasion the consensus was that it had fallen outside the wire, and the only casualty was our sleep.

Later in the day we went and found our audience, hiding in plain sight in a corner of the camp looking like just another vehicle park, and gave our brief. Clearly these guys were thoroughly switched on, as the few questions we had to field all made sense, and they showed their appreciation by inviting us back to Sunday dinner later in the evening. We were slightly conflicted, as this camp was notoriously catered for by everything from Pizza Express to Dunkin' Donuts and our hosts' facilities did not look very promising.

But it would have been rude to refuse, so having spent the afternoon visiting the famous 'Boardwalk', an enormous US-style mall in the middle of camp, resisting the fast food temptations on all sides, we returned with grumbling tummies to the 'vehicle park', full of dubious anticipation. Then we learnt that our world-famous SF enjoy skills well beyond just killing the Queen's enemies with ruthless efficiency, as we were treated to a fantastic roast with all the trimmings. I'm sure they had a well-stocked bar discreetly tucked away as well, but if so, they very sensibly kept it to themselves. On the way back to our bunks we all agreed that it had been by far the best meal any of us had had in the country.

By mid-December the weather up at the airport was starting to get seriously cold and every morning the view of the mountains got prettier and the walk to work sludgier as the snow cover increased. The TOC team and I had time for one more road trip before Christmas.

This time we were headed out to a very remote location which was a bit more of a mission than our previous visits, and took a while. Our destination was FOB Salerno, located in the eastern Khost province. This was only fifteen miles from the border with the Pakistan badlands known as the Federally Administered Tribal Area, home to a number of radical Islamic Madrassas,[25] and very close to the notorious Tora Bora cave complex where Bin Laden had narrowly evaded capture back in 2002.

This area, serviced only by the narrow ambush alley known as the Khost-Gardez pass, had often been the scene of heavy fighting over the years, not just for ISAF but also the Soviets before them. Salerno was named by the US 505 Parachute Infantry Regiment who were the first to take up residence, after their predecessors' September 1943 airborne beachhead assault in Italy and was now home to nearly 3,000 mainly US troops.

First, we took the short flight across the capital down to Bagram, which I had previously visited during my recce a little over a year before. I had forgotten how enormous the place was and when we got there it was as busy as Gatwick on Boxing Day. There was a fair bit of shuffling around and indecision about the next leg of the trip but finally, as night fell, we settled in a chilly waiting area among rows of Black Hawk and Chinook helicopters. After an hour or so we were joined by a platoon of travelling companions from a US unit based in Alaska who had just arrived to take up their twelve-month posting at FOB Salerno with Task Force Duke. The US mission deployment bureaucracy was tortuous at the best of times but hearing the tale of their journey so far, I felt for them, as it had already been two weeks since they left home.

It was a perfect storm of logistical demands, with the normal Christmas churn of movements, the 10,000-man drawdown from Afghanistan and the knock-on effect of a short notice deadline of 18 December for the last US troops to be out of Iraq, following failure to negotiate a satisfactory SOFA there.[26] These poor guys' first stop after Anchorage had been Leipzig (why?) where they were stuck for four days, then Manas in Uzbekistan for another three or four and now several more days hanging about in Bagram with only a tantalizing 150 or so miles to go. Needless to say, they were already exhausted.

Two of the Chinooks eventually coughed into life and the movements staff divided our waiting group between them. It was a tight squeeze in the aircraft with baggage piled all down the centre, because although we were travelling light, our companions were not, and everybody was bulked up like Michelin men, with cold-weather kit, weapons, full body armour, helmets and goggles. This sardine-like arrangement did at least keep us nice and warm for a while, but it didn't stay that way for long once we had gained altitude, mainly because there was a machine-gunner stationed at an open porthole on each side of the front of the helicopter.

It was of course very noisy, and soon also became very cold indeed but it was an exciting trip; a surreal sensation completed by the protective facemasks worn by the door gunners. They were made of some sort of white plastic, so that they looked exactly like Star Wars Imperial stormtroopers; this surely cannot have been a design coincidence. I did a double-take when I first saw them: was this a helicopter or the 'Death Star'?

Looking down, once we had yet again left Kabul behind us, it felt as if there would have been more signs of life from the air on the dark side of the moon. This impression was hardly dispelled when we landed in what appeared to be the middle of nowhere at about 1.30 am, after a little over an hour of this assault on the senses. We were then escorted to our accommodation, itself an interesting experience, given that the entire camp was totally blacked out both inside and outside the buildings.

Getting to bed consequently involved a fair amount of blundering about and bad language but having finally found an empty one without quite waking the entire dorm or losing all my kit, I slept pretty well, after what had been a full-on day. I later discovered that there hadn't been a power cut as I had assumed, but the camp was blacked out every night to discourage the locals from mortar and rocket attacks which were a regular occurrence in these parts, where there probably wasn't that much else to do at night.

Despite, or perhaps because of, its remoteness, I enjoyed the environment way out here. For the first time since I had arrived in July, I went for something approaching a country walk, as the camp perimeter was remarkably open, at least during the day. The morning was very fresh and clear but even in mid-December it warmed up to a very pleasant temperature later on.

The country actually looked a bit greener than elsewhere, complete with mynah birdlife and orange groves for a change. The only disturbance on my walk was caused by a bunch of Afghan army recruits in training. It was very clear that drill was not a natural talent in these parts, and I couldn't help wondering whether in the circumstances 'marching up and down' was much of a priority.

Inside camp the benefits of an infrastructure which was not permanently stressed by excessive numbers like IJC were obvious, with an excellent gym and washing and dining facilities. There were lots of American soldiers out jogging in regimented squads, wearing uniform grey army PT kit, rounded off with 'hi viz' belts, presumably to avoid being run over in broad daylight by APCs crawling about at 30 kph. Apart from the suntanned extremities they looked exactly as I remembered them back in Fort Lewis, Seattle, but this seemed an incongruous place for an 'elf 'n' safety' obsession. What a contrast to British squaddies, who tend to jog in pairs, looking rather smaller and scruffier.

We then spent three successive days giving our standard brief, first to an audience of newly arrived young American soldiers and quite a few officers, all of whom were impeccably polite, intelligent and appreciative. On day two there were some very bright JAG officers among them which made a nice change as it involved some interesting dialogue to break up the lecturing.

I was really in no great rush to get back to KAIA, which was just as well as it turned out, as it was becoming clear that just getting around the country was often a drama despite the substantial number of multinational military aircraft about. However, it was almost Christmas Eve and I did at least want to be back amongst my colleagues for some sort of celebration. So, on the evening of 23 December, I was standing on a clinker airstrip under brilliant stars (no light pollution out here), enjoying the warm back draught, if not the noise, from a Herc' 'turning and burning' in front of me, waiting for a flight back out.

We were only thirty minutes' direct flying time from KAIA but no such luck. First, it was a half-hour flight up to Bagram, delayed by nearly eight hours, arriving about midnight, and a further delay there of another six hours before walking out to another Herc in about −9°C of early morning, brilliant winter sun, climbing aboard for the fifteen-minute trip back up to KAIA.

So much for my inevitably rather remote input to the kinetic end of the operational spectrum, the 'kill' part of the 'kill or capture' options for the ISAF counterinsurgency mission. In some ways, at least for soldiers on the ground, killing is the easy bit – you are on patrol, you are engaged by the enemy, a firefight develops and hopefully you survive. Subsequently an intelligence report will probably provide a reasonably accurate enemy body count, but your attention by then is on your next patrol, not who may have killed whom.

Capturing the enemy is a much longer story.

Prisoner handling on military operations has always been logistically very demanding but nowadays it is also every bit as problematic from a legal point of view. The strategic damage done to US operations in Iraq following the Abu Ghraib scandal, compounded subsequently by their controversial Guantanamo Bay policies, is hard to overestimate. The UK also had its share of problems on that operation, such as the notorious case of Baha Mousa who died in military custody in Basra in 2003, resulting in the court martial of a number of soldiers from the Queens Lancashire Regiment, including the CO.

It is a worrying irony that, for soldiers, that entirely proper legal scrutiny of prisoner handling inevitably sometimes makes killing the enemy a much simpler and more attractive option than capturing him. Little did I know that on 15 September, when I had been in Kabul for a couple of months, down in Helmand Province Royal Marine Sergeant Blackman had decided it would be a better idea to kill his severely wounded Taliban captive by shooting him in the chest than go through the dangerous process of organizing his evacuation.

This came to light months later during a review of 'helmet cam' evidence of the scene, in which Blackman could be heard warning his comrades to keep quiet about it because he had breached the Geneva Conventions.[27] After initially being convicted of murder, he was extremely fortunate to have his conviction reduced to manslaughter on appeal. One can only speculate whether this incident was just the tip of an iceberg, and if so, how big.[28]

The US 'exceptional' view of human rights during armed conflict allowed their personnel a greater degree of freedom of action but following the Iraq experience and various judgments of the European Court of Human Rights, the UK had learnt the lesson that wherever in the world her armed forces operate they must apply the ECHR to those over whom they have effective control. This presented a real challenge in Afghanistan, where British soldiers frequently took Taliban prisoners.

As the prospect of ISAF drawing down and handing off security to the ANSF drew ever closer, joint ISAF/ANA patrols became the norm. One cunning plan for the prisoner problem was to ensure that on such patrols it was the Afghans who did the capturing in the first place, not the Brits, thus exonerating the latter from any subsequent human rights abuses. This was frowned upon as a transparent legal device, quite apart from the fact that the ANA would often not bother to question their prisoners at all, and at worst – quite often – simply release them forthwith.

The Convention severely restricted the time for which prisoners could be held before either being released or handed over to the Afghan authorities.[29] With the clock ticking from point of capture, this ensured a major headache in gathering potentially vital intelligence from them. The difficulty did not end there, however, because if the Afghan police, NDS[30] and prison systems fell short of the Convention's expectations in their treatment of prisoners handed over to them by the UK, the UK arguably still remained legally responsible. In a country whose prison system was notoriously primitive[31] this was a nightmare waiting to happen.

The UK's solution devised for this riddle was to establish something called the (imaginatively titled?) Detention Oversight Team (DOT), comprising an ALS lieutenant-colonel and a Royal Military Police (RMP) major. Based at Camp Bastion, the sprawling UK HQ in Helmand Province, successive teams spent an entire six-month tour of duty visiting a variety of Afghan prisons interviewing prisoners to ensure, as far as possible, that their human rights were being respected to European standards, and if not, making the necessary representations.

This was a dangerous and unenviable task, involving constant road travel through hostile territory, often to find an equally hostile reception from prison management who resented the intrusion on their domain, let alone criticism, and dealing with prisoners whose gratitude for this attention, if any, was trumped by their visceral hatred of their infidel captors. As a NATO staff officer my involvement with the team, headed at the time by my ALS friend Nigel Heppenstall, was no more than occasionally to provide moral support. They, and those who came before and after them did that difficult job remarkably well, as evidenced by the minimal amount of litigation arising, unlike in Iraq – a lesson well learnt.

ISAF was not the only UN-sanctioned mission in Afghanistan. Since early 2002 a complementary civilian UN body, the UN Assistance Mission in Afghanistan (UNAMA), had been working alongside us. The mission reported annually on developments and during early autumn 2011 a substantial leak indicated that their imminent report on Afghan prison arrangements was likely to be something of a bombshell for ISAF.

General Allen was clearly seriously rattled by the UNAMA leak and a conference was convened at IJC – held for some bizarre reason in the Christian chapel – to consider ISAF's options in response, assuming the dreaded report was as damning as was feared. The star turn was a reservist US colonel whose day job was as a civilian prison official back home. He described the culture of Afghan jails, to keep prisoners in horrendously hot and overcrowded conditions and, in his words 'beat the shit out of them' to secure confessions.

Favourite methods included 'genital manipulation', hanging from the ceiling, electrocution, beating with rubber hoses, in fact ... you name it. Kids often went to live in jail with their imprisoned parents, having nowhere else to go, and it was quite normal for other relatives to visit with gifts of 'half a cow' or bunches of watermelons, which then turned out to be stuffed with such treats as large wraps of heroin, pistols and mobile phones. Disease was rife and medical treatment basic, with the 'isolation cell' for those with TB in one prison being the roof of the latrines.

When the report was finally formally released a couple of weeks later it had been so comprehensively leaked that there were few real surprises. It seemed that certainly in some instances the good colonel at the conference had been spot on, with an interrogator in one case memorably quoted: 'You will confess, even stones confess here' and another senior official admitting, 'Yes, sure it happens, confessions are very important to judges in this country and sometimes that [beatings or torture] is the only way we get them.'

I could not help wondering what the human rights court in Strasbourg would have had to say about that, but it would of course be completely mistaken to assume that criminal systems throughout the world are comfortable and familiar with Western notions of evidence. In Afghanistan judges were wary of third party, even eyewitness, evidence because of the fear and/or corruption by which it was more often than not distorted. Written evidence, in a largely illiterate society reliant on oral narrative, was treated with suspicion, and they had no means of understanding or interpreting modern scientific, forensic evidence. Hence the paramount importance of confessions.

Being deployed in the livelier operational areas of the country, the US and the UK were responsible for the vast majority of insurgents arrested and handed over but fortunately, largely because of the effectiveness of the DOT process, few British-captured detainees were problematic. For once we had stolen a march on our big brother ally, who had no DOT equivalent and as events developed, they found themselves wishing they had.

The commander's initial plan was to carry on handing prisoners over on an undertaking from the Afghans that they would not be mistreated.

This may have seemed straightforward but it was immediately clear that it would not wash with UNAMA, not least because the Afghan government denied that anybody anywhere was being mistreated.

However, the formal release of the report did at least give us the names of the worst establishments, and so began the monumental task of 'sanitizing' ISAF's prisoner handling throughout the country. This fell to the provost branch at IJC, a small and hitherto fairly relaxed office led by my friend Colonel Pat Cairns, ably assisted by his SO2, Major Keith Scott. They were both British RMP officers but most of their inexperienced support staff were little more than passengers, so between them they suddenly had their work cut out.

Overnight they found themselves working 24/7 to try and log where every single prisoner originally captured by ISAF anywhere in the country was being held, compare it with the UNAMA list of 'tainted' establishments and arrange moves to safe, alternative prisons where necessary. ISAF could just about deal with those on remand awaiting trial but for those who had already been convicted and sentenced matters were out of our hands. At the same time, urgent arrangements had to be made to ensure that from that point on nobody was sent to any of the 'wrong' places. The whole process was an extremely unwelcome operation lasting many weeks, which not only involved time-consuming staff effort but also complex, sometimes clandestine and often potentially dangerous, mass movements of prisoners.

There were two crucial differences between Afghanistan in 2011 and Abu Ghraib a few years before. First, all of Afghanistan was a seriously hostile environment for even the most intrepid photo-journalist, and secondly, whilst Abu Ghraib had been staffed by occasionally careless, leaky, or indeed remorseful US service personnel with cameras, the Afghan prisons were not. This was fortunate for General Allen, who was understandably in fear of Afghanistan's own Abu Ghraib scandal erupting on his watch and he demanded detailed daily progress reports on all of the provost branch's work. Even after this immediate crisis had been addressed the difficulties of detainee handling continued.

Any underlying, unspoken bias for soldiers to kill rather than capture is perhaps an example of perfection being the enemy of sufficiency – an unintended consequence of expecting Western notions of human rights to fix the stricken lives of people everywhere.

Chapter 8

Hearts and Minds

'The ultimate victory will depend on the hearts and minds of the people who actually live out there.'
President L. B. Johnson, Texas 1965 on the Vietnam War

Killing or capturing the enemy are the oldest and bluntest weapons in the combatant's armoury but in recent times politicians and generals alike have come to appreciate the value of another, the people's psyche.

The origins of the deliberate addition of winning 'hearts and minds' to conventional military objectives in battle are disputed but they certainly go back to French campaigning in Indo China in the nineteenth century and the British in Malaya in the 1950s. By the time ISAF and the civilian UNAMA mission kicked off, the US had already been struggling for many years to win hearts and minds in Iraq and although this met with little more success than it had in Vietnam, it was a challenge that had to be addressed in Afghanistan too.

The military campaign ebbed and flowed according to factors which were at least somewhat predictable, such as the Taliban's summer 'fighting season' followed by winter retrenchment. The psychological operation, however difficult to plan, had to be maintained at all times and at all levels, from strategic messaging to tactical sensitivity.

General Scaparotti clearly knew what the 'hearts and minds' concept was all about, as demonstrated when he hosted an *Iftar*, a Muslim evening breakfast during Ramadan up at IJC, but it could well have ended in tears. The Afghan dignitaries were hosted in one of the DFACs, and their drivers were given a packed meal in the carpark. However, despite their day's fasting they turned their noses up at the soggy sandwiches, which had been in the fridge too long, and became restless. The system then relented, and they too were invited up to the DFAC. They arrived mob-handed, and armed to the teeth, much to the dismay of various senior ISAF officers' and dignitaries' CP teams, realizing that if anything kicked off, they would be hopelessly outgunned. It all sounded rather rash, given the tendency of the ANA from time to time to forget whose side they are supposed to be on.

But the pièce de résistance was the NASCAR[1]-style departure of the guests' convoy of 4x4s at the close of play. The idea was that they would leave in some sort of prioritized order, through the single-lane security corridor leading from the HQ along the perimeter to the gate. But the drivers had other ideas, and, as if on a starting grid, the moment the first vehicle was waved on by the Mongolian security man every engine started up and the evening air was filled with the roar and fumes of diesel engines, with drivers competing as if in a Buzkashi match[2] to force their vehicle ahead of the next through the single exit point. Still, it seemed that fun was had by all in the end and the day could be counted as a public relations success.

One of our biggest headaches was how to address the matter of narcotics. Afghanistan has for many years supplanted the Southeast Asian 'Golden Triangle' as the world's most prolific poppy grower, and like cocaine for the FARC in Colombia, heroin production is the Taliban's money tree. Destruction of the poppy crop was consequently identified as a legitimate counterinsurgency tool as well as, less controversially, a counter-narcotics activity of benefit to the world at large.

The elephant in this room, however, was that in many parts of rural Afghanistan poppy farming is a matter of survival, the only commercial show in town. On the one hand ISAF was pouring money into PRTs in order to revive the rural economy and win over the hearts and minds of the people to renounce the lure of the insurgency, and on the other they were systematically destroying their only means of making a living. Attempts to introduce alternatives like cereal or even saffron literally just ran into the sand, and this problem remains unsolved to this day.

Whereas poppy eradication could be viewed as being almost deliberately provocative and counterproductive in the hearts and minds campaign, from time to time ISAF inevitably also made other mistakes. These typically involved excessive or careless use of force, killing either our own allies or civilians,[3] and the enemy were increasingly adept at seizing the narrative to their own advantage on these occasions, hence the zero-tolerance regime for collateral deaths.

ISAF had to find a way to get ahead of the PR game following such incidents and one effective part of the solution, in addition to the occasional 'tiger team', was another inquiry procedure called Joint Incident Assessment Teams, or JIATs.

The 'joint' bit meant that, in order to demonstrate transparency, the team always included at least one Afghan government representative, usually uniformed, alongside the ISAF personnel. They were called 'assessment' rather than investigation teams because the word 'investigation' is usually associated with criminal matters and it was felt that they were less likely to get at the truth if witnesses believed they might be under some form of criminal investigation. There was still always the possibility that such incidents would lead to disciplinary or criminal prosecution, so the difficult trick was to produce a frank and detailed report without either frightening witnesses off or doing anything which could prejudice such proceedings later.

The teams, which were supposed to deploy within twenty-four hours of the incident in order to keep ahead of the Taliban's own agile PR, were often set up by IJC, typically led by a brigadier and always including a legal officer and a PR representative, alongside whatever other interpreters and subject matter experts were needed.

Either by luck or perhaps because the use of force really was pretty well under control, we sent out very few JIATs during my time but just when you thought there was real progress being made, some mediaeval cruelty would come to light.

One day in early October we received a report from up north of a group of Afghan policemen dragging a prisoner along the ground on a chain behind a motorbike; he was dead before anybody could intervene. This was nothing to do with ISAF but because it had been witnessed and reported by a US unit, it was important to ensure that fact went on the record, so we sent a JIAT up, with Katy as the legal advisor. History does not record the outcome, sadly probably of no consequence, given the dubious state of Afghan police discipline but at least for once ISAF's reputation was fairly safe.

Whereas JIATs were purely reactive, the PRTs, with projects as varied as building schools, repairing dams[4] and trying to establish the administration of a more sophisticated justice than that meted out by the Taliban throughout the country, were a dangerous, labour-intensive but thoroughly worthy operational tool. However, their success varied enormously according to factors usually beyond their control, such as local demographics, which warlords ruled the roost, whether they were in a poppy-growing region and how many 'night raids'[5] special forces were conducting in the area.

Two paragraphs describing two different issues in my diary on one day illustrate how insoluble some of the 'hearts and minds' problems were, becoming no easier, in fact if anything getting harder as time went on:

> Jen [one of our JAG captains] had compiled a history of the sorry tale of U.S. land acquisition at Bagram over the last 5 years or so, during which a combination of confused legal advice and local cunning seems to have had them running round in circles wasting money paying the wrong people rent, and antagonizing others. It should be straightforward, as the Military Technical Agreement provides that they shouldn't be paying rent, and where any rent or compensation for land use is payable it should be the Afghan Gov't which pays it. In this instance the latter have consistently defaulted, so I feel a little sorry for successive U.S. commanders who have been over a barrel. Anyway, it's really an HQ ISAF matter, but interesting to have an insight.
>
> I also watched a VTC from the NATO Training Mission Afghanistan (NTMA) about Rule of Law which was pretty interesting. It confirmed the place is basically a zoo, with lots of different police forces with no idea of how to police people, and mainly concerned with their own security (not surprising perhaps, as they are the Aunt Sallys around here). Nobody talks to each other who needs to, e.g. the Ministries, the police, the courts etc etc, and legislation is either bad, outdated, or stalled. All pretty depressing for the future of this country, and our mission!

The old adage that, 'money doesn't just talk, it yells out loud' clearly applied every bit as much here as anywhere else. Despite the evident difficulty of settling real estate claims, one effective operational tool in which our little legal office played a major role was dealing with other financial claims against ISAF.

I discovered on arrival that although each ISAF nation had its own individual claims procedure, they varied considerably from having zero budget to extreme generosity, predictably dependent on the wealth of the nation in question. ISAF also had a joint claims office, which we ran at IJC, and having had experience of something similar back in Kosovo, I took it on. Our little team did all the prep in the office and went downtown to HQ ISAF every week to assess new claimants in person and settle those matters which were ready.

My diary goes on to recall my first visit one day in late July:

> In the P.M. we actually went out on the street to receive the claimants in the hot sun, amidst a gaggle of scruffy and undisciplined Afghan National Army guards. The claimants were a very motley and dodgy bunch, principally claiming for RTAs in which they alleged they had lost their horse, funnily enough the preferred beast to lose (presumably because much more valuable than any other) although you hardly ever see a horse about, mainly goats and donkeys, or their car, which was invariably for some reason a Toyota Corolla. It's fair to say about 75% of the cars on the streets, other than the ubiquitous armoured 4x4s driven by military, NGOs, UN and Gov't officials, are indeed Toyota Corollas. We had difficulty getting an accurate valuation for a horse, but the nearest we could get for a Corolla was in Peshawar, Pakistan, where a fifteen-year-old one is apparently valued at about $15,000 U.S., or £9,000, which seems amazing, but might explain again why they are a popular choice to claim as a write-off.
>
> In fairness some of the claims are undoubtedly genuine, albeit probably laced with a degree of contributory negligence, but although in many cases the responsible nation can be identified (many French cases in the Sarobi area near Kabul, for example) not only do military drivers tend to drive straight on due to security fears (fair enough),[6] but even if they accept liability they will not pay out as their national law forbids it, and the claim has to come to our ISAF system, which is pretty limited, particularly in funds, which amount to $200,000 PA.
>
> We had one classic black-bearded, hook-nosed Afghan chap on crutches with a well-documented case in which one of his sons was the car driver, and was killed, another had

suffered brain damage, and the claimant had been knocked unconscious and couldn't remember what happened. Amazingly the driver's licence was on file, showing an appalling record, which suggested it was probably his fault, in fact I suspect driving on drugs. In any event the claimant, who turned out to be a doctor, and who had been paying his son as his driver said he had lost everything, but had difficulty grasping the notion of producing evidence of causation.

Another very well-fed and hulking but soft-spoken farmer turned up with a sweet little brown Afghan hat on, brandishing a piece of paper with a Pashtu statement from some Ministry apparently proving his ownership of some land, with an ISAF dispute. Apparently, he turns up week after week with such pieces of paper, only to be told we don't do land claims.

Another young chap claimed his horse had been run over and killed by a 'tank' while being shod in the blacksmiths. First it was a stallion, then it was a mare then it turned out to be 'on the way to; the blacksmiths, and so the tale kept changing.

Most of those who were turned away were philosophical, realizing that despite a good try, especially for generally poor and illiterate people, they had been found out, and that was it, but some turned quite nasty, and had to be firmly told by the guards to sling their hook. It was not the ideal setting for such dealings and my strong recommendation for the future will be to conduct these interviews in the security of the camp, for those whose case is sufficient to be allowed in.

We only actually paid one claim today, for about $200, and had the recipient stand in front of a door holding the notes in front of him with the sum, name, and date written on the door while we took a photo of the collage as proof of payment. I learnt later in the day that the fund only has $38,000 left for the year until January, so we may struggle. I believe we should be as generous as possible in genuine cases, as these people do not ask ISAF to come and run them or their stock over and ruin their lives, they have no such thing as motor insurance, and if we don't do the right thing we cannot be surprised if they turn their back on us, assuming they don't hate us enough already. The false claims are not too hard to weed out, and the sums involved mean everything to these poor bastards but are the tiniest drop in the ocean of what nations are spending out here, largely to kill people.

Chris Knight, who was our main claims workhorse, later regaled us with the story of a claimant on another occasion who had lost his pride and joy, a brand-new Corolla, under the tracks of an APC. He said he had run out of fuel because he hadn't understood what the fuel gauge did, and gone off with a can for a top-up, only to find the car flattened when he returned – one of those tales which sounded so unlikely it was probably true.

I found it very useful to discover from this early trip downtown just how the system worked as I came home following our two days there with some firm views about ways to improve matters. First, I was quite alarmed at how little cash we were apparently proposing to devote to this, and persuaded the budget holders that our methodology should not rely on mitigating each claim with an eye to dwindling funds but allow an honest and reasonable assessment of the merit and value of each claim and pay accordingly, expanding the budget as necessary.

These were severely impoverished people and although in many cases their notion of integrity left much to be desired, there were others with genuine and serious grievances. Proper and generous handling of those matters was a force multiplier for us which we should not overlook.

Secondly, I was very concerned about security. The claims team had for months been operating as I saw them, showing up as regular as clockwork every Wednesday afternoon, lightly armed, in the street outside the ISAF perimeter in the presence of random 'fighting age' Afghans, all of whom either had genuine personal reasons for disliking us, hence their claim, or with a dishonest intent to defraud us. The only security apart from our own sidearms was the leaky Green Zone 'ring of steel' and the hopeless ANA guard and it seemed to me that the odds of somebody one day turning up with a concealed weapon or a suicide vest and a violent grievance when his claim was rejected were unacceptably short.

Hearts and Minds

From then on, we made arrangements with security at HQ ISAF to operate inside the wire, with claimants vetted and searched before being admitted under escort, for assessment and/or payment and then escorted back off the premises.

In 1906, another US president, Theodore Roosevelt, said, 'If you've got them by the balls their hearts and minds will follow.' Perhaps ISAF's biggest problem was that it never did manage to secure that part of the Afghan people's anatomy, although even had it succeeded in doing so, I have my doubts whether in their case the principle would have applied.

Poor old Afghanistan, a country so internally divided by tribalism and the remoteness of most of the population from the capital that no government of its own seems capable of ruling by any sort of national consensus. It seemed to me that sadly, despite our best efforts, those who seriously believed a Western, almost exclusively Christian coalition like ISAF stood any chance of winning the 'hearts and minds' battle in this wild and unruly country were living in 'La La Land'.

Epilogue

Justitia in Armis

The motto of the Army Legal Service, loosely translated as 'Justice in Arms', covers a multitude of sins. The legal practice described on these pages is just one of them, generally referred to as 'operational law', itself a portfolio term covering everything from the *ius ad bellum* to General Order No. 1.

Until relatively recently, the business of justice in arms in the British armed forces almost exclusively referred to military discipline. The core skills demanded of military lawyers were familiarity with the provisions of the service discipline Acts[1] in order to advise the chain of command on disciplinary and criminal matters, preparation of cases for trial and prosecution on behalf of the Crown at courts martial. Operational law was very much a 'minor sport', the hobby horse of one or two individuals who were generally regarded with a degree of bemused suspicion.

Criminal prosecution is hard work, demanding not only great expertise in the relevant laws and procedures but long hours of meticulous preparation and the mental agility to 'think on your feet', with nowhere to hide during trial, in the presence of skilled opponents and sometimes very bad-tempered judges. As a prosecutor, the rules of evidence under English law are heavily stacked against you and as soon as the stress of one case is over, whatever the verdict, you are immediately immersed in the next, with little time either to celebrate or lick your wounds.

As if that wasn't enough to contend with, the military prosecutor also tends to suffer from a diet of work which is extremely procedure and preparation heavy, with relatively intermittent appearances in court. On the other hand, their opponents at the civilian Bar are well accustomed to spending five days a week in the Crown Courts, with much of their prep undertaken by instructing solicitors.

Practitioners in this specialized work are justly proud of what they do, and there is a school of thought that court-martial prosecution is the military lawyer's 'front line'.

It's not a competition, but having been both a military prosecutor and an operational lawyer, I beg to differ.

There is an argument that in peacetime it is indeed the administrators, like the paymasters, the padres, the medics and the lawyers, who are the only ones doing real jobs, dealing with real illnesses and real crimes and keeping the whole show on the road all the time, while the soldiers are just at play, doing just that, 'playing soldiers', training for something that may never happen.

But the raison d'être of the armed forces is not to go to work on the ranges or in the pay office, the surgery or the court martial centre; it is, ultimately, to close with the Queen's enemies wherever they may be, and, if necessary, kill them.

Everything else is peripheral, the tail, not the dog.

So, when that does happen, the work of those medics and padres and yes, even the lawyers, can make the difference between victory and defeat. Many of them would be a good deal further forward than I was, relatively junior officers in the thick of it alongside the 'steely-eyed killers', working incredibly long hours while living in some danger and discomfort rather than returning home to the safety of their own beds at night. Even without the benefit of experience or seniority to bolster their confidence, they are frequently called upon to give life or death advice to commanders many ranks above them – it can be pretty lonely.

My frustration in Kosovo with the apparent inability of some staff further up the chain to appreciate what was actually happening on the ground and provide practical support must be evident from my account. Sometimes this is aggravated by differing national positions within an alliance such as NATO, at others the friction is more a matter of politics within the national hierarchy,[2] or the problem may simply be the lack of imagination of those enjoying the normality of life far to the rear.[3]

For all the availability of modern communications, like others before me and no doubt after me, I was struck by this yawning disconnect between those actually in the theatre of operations and those not, and in Kabul I was well behind those lawyers out in the regional commands.

To a degree, the lawyers have become victims of their own success in the world of operational law. In recent years British commanders have frequently declared quite openly that they will not deploy on operations without a lawyer 'in their pocket', a very far cry from the Falklands situation during the first few months of my service. Sometimes in Kabul we found we were having to 'triage' those matters in which we would become involved, such was the demand for some legal 'cover'.

Legal advice is understandably seen as a tangible example of the precautions which military commanders now know they must take to guard against immediate strategic pitfalls or damaging litigation downstream.

The demand for lawyers with different skills fluctuates with changing times in the armed services as in any other market. The demise of the USSR liberated the UN Security Council, so that previously unthinkable resolutions authorizing a range of military operations could now pass. Thus, much of the increased demand for lawyers in the British Army during my career occurred because of the growing number of military operations which took place over those years, combined with the world's concurrent growing awareness of the rights of those caught up in them.

Ironically, that very same geopolitical upheaval in the early 1990s eventually enabled the British Army to slash its overseas garrisons, already reduced by withdrawal from empire, so the need for the expeditionary court-martial structure has diminished, and with it the demand for military prosecutors.

My crystal ball suggests that for the foreseeable future the demand for armed services lawyers may be greater in other fields again, such as domestic employment law, human rights and other less classically 'military' areas.

For the uniformed lawyer to guarantee survival, therefore, it seems to me operational law is the only way ahead. Unlike a civilian, his uniform not only provides the credibility he needs in the field, but it also requires him to go where and when he is sent, however dangerous or uncomfortable, like any other soldier, whereas any suitably qualified lawyer in a suit can prosecute a burglary in Bulford or a criminal damage in Catterick.

As for NATO, it's been a while for me, but a glance at the map of Europe suggests that perhaps the flurry of expansion eastwards, together with the PfP satellite countries, has reached its limit. Having said that, I did hear talk of Australia making friendly noises – now that would surely be the ultimate mission creep.

However, with nerve agent in Salisbury and annexation in the Crimea some might argue that things have not really changed much since that night at Sandhurst over thirty years ago, where this story began.

Endnotes

Introduction

1. It has been unkindly suggested that this was in itself an historic occasion.
2. Francis Fukuyama, *The End of History and the Last Man* (Free Press 1992).
3. The Washington Treaty 1949.
4. GC I Art 47, GC II Art 48, GC III Art 127, GC IV 4 Art 144 – 'The High Contracting Parties undertake … to disseminate the text of the present Convention as widely as possible.'
5. Art 82 – 'The High Contracting Parties … shall ensure that legal advisers are available, when necessary, to advise military commanders at the appropriate level on the application of the Conventions and this Protocol and on the appropriate instruction to be given to the armed forces on this subject'.

Chapter 1: On Her Majesty's Legal Service

1. A former base in the Maldives, now Gan International, it was said to be populated at that time by over 1,000 servicemen and one postmistress, a very popular lady.
2. Which gained fame the same year in *The Man with the Golden Gun*, having also been the scene of the surrender of the colony to the Japanese on Christmas Day, 1941.
3. You could only see the contents by peering into the top and I well remember trying to get away with a ginger beer when the Royal Welch QM did just that and insisted, ''Ave a proper bloody drink, boyo!'
4. The courteous form of address was traditionally reciprocated between British and Gurkha officers, pronounced Saab, like the Swedish car.

5. OPs of course in army-speak.
6. Known as 'Jock the Sock'.
7. Such as Terry Jack's 'Seasons in the Sun', Paper Lace's 'Billy Don't Be a Hero' (an army favourite!) and Charlie Rich's 'The Most Beautiful Girl in the World'.
8. Which was to become the Army Legal Corps in 1979.
9. Aide-de-camp.
10. Anglo-French diplomacy at its finest.
11. Sir David Attenborough.
12. Everybody stank like polecats within a day of this, although it was not apparent until you'd got back to Tutong at the end of three or four days out, showered and then met someone else coming back who hadn't yet done so!
13. Six out of the then ten Gurkha regiments remained in the new Indian Army.
14. Several thousand Gurkhas apply for about 200 vacancies each year.
15. The notorious Menus A, B, C or D.
16. From an Assamese word for a thatched shelter.
17. Unit Motor Transport section.
18. Paul Scott 1965–1975.
19. Trainee solicitors have always spent at least two years in practice before qualifying. During this period, now called a training contract, they used to be known as 'articled clerks'.
20. Barristers' twelve-month equivalent of articles of clerkship.
21. This bit didn't disappoint.
22. I can't even remember what that meant.
23. The only specific field of law covered during my degree course in which I continue to practise today, and an essential speciality in military operational law.
24. With the exception of my sadly missed Omega, which had been ripped from my wrist and presumably discarded when I gave chase.
25. A very impressive 'flash to bang' time which if only modern English Crown Courts could manage, between offence and trial.
26. A legal procedure long since abandoned under the English law of criminal evidence whereby the witness could be asked to say whether he could identify the accused in court. This was obviously highly prejudicial because the witness would be bound to know that the guy in the dock is the suspect, whether he truly recognizes him or not.

Endnotes

27. An Old Etonian and one of the last white judges in Kenya, who, having had an interesting war in the SOE, had settled in Kenya instead of returning to the London Bar. He had been active in anti-Mau Mau operations in the 1950s. We learnt a couple of years after our visit that he had been murdered at his home by a burglar.
28. Who seemed quite impressed, but warned me not to have it published in my own name if I envisaged returning to Kenya any time soon – a proud accolade.
29. A white South African lawyer, who had been imprisoned for anti-apartheid activities and publications by the apartheid regime there before coming to England.
30. In those days most people got a 2:2, variously known as a gentleman's degree, a sportsman's degree or a 'Desmond'.
31. Which we sat in the freezing cold Alexandra Palace, the 'Ally Pally', in north London.
32. The Law Society's recommended minimum.
33. The Law Society's recommended minimum for the second year in articles!
34. John Taylor was by then back in UK as a lieutenant-colonel and, in his new role as SO1 to the Director ALC, officiated at my interview. He retired some years ago as a brigadier.
35. Under AP1 Art 43.2 chaplains are non-combatants and although there is no specific prohibition on their bearing arms they are not permitted to participate directly in hostilities. It would therefore be embarrassing if some enterprising journalist with an axe to grind were to snap a chaplain blasting away on the ranges, which could then be photoshopped into a war zone.
36. Royal Ulster Constabulary, the predecessors of today's Police Service of Northern Ireland.
37. A Westland Helicopter, a design long since retired.
38. An 'out of bounds' route from HQNI in Lisburn to Londonderry in the west which knocked half an hour off the journey by the safer coast road.
39. A Humber armoured car, so named because it was very ugly.
40. Thus, counter-intuitively, bright green meant danger and bright orange meant safe.
41. The Director Army Legal Services, a 2* appointment. ALC had become ALS by this time.

42. The International Criminal Tribunal for the former Yugoslavia. This was the ad hoc court set up in the Hague to try war crimes committed during the Balkans war in the 1990s. ALS had a major on the staff, about to be upgraded to lieutenant-colonel.
43. Now a QC, recently appointed Her Majesty's Chief Inspector of the Crown Prosecution Service.
44. Sometimes known as 'sinking the ship in the harbour'.
45. The Allied Rapid Reaction Corps.

Chapter 2: *Audentis Fortuna Iuvat*

1. The only time Art. 5 has ever been invoked to date was following the attacks on the US on 9 September 2001. All other NATO operations are simply referred to for legal purposes as 'Non Article 5'.
2. Some of them via the Partnership for Peace treaty programme launched in 1994 as a means of transition to full NATO membership.
3. Strictly speaking in NATO-speak a 'High Readiness Force (Land)'.
4. Whose ADC invariably produced the best cup of coffee in the HQ, naturally.
5. Supreme Headquarters Allied Powers Europe.
6. In fact, we even boasted Legionnaire's disease from time to time.
7. This was rather spooky déjà vu for me, as the motto of Wellington College is *Virtutis Fortuna Comes* which translates as 'Fortune Favours the Bold'. I wonder if this is a coincidence or did one of the many O.W. senior British army officers over the years have a hand in it?
8. A successful model for additional HRFs in later years.
9. For some nations the allowances paid in NATO appointments are quite substantial relative to national pay scales.
10. On more than one occasion I only just stopped myself in time from addressing other lieutenant-colonels as 'Colonel' and saluting them, as I had been used to doing for so many years.
11. This would be a war crime if applied to the enemy, but not amongst your own staff officers!
12. Staff Officer, Grade 2.
13. Mike Maples, a really likeable man who went on to become Director, US Defense Intelligence Agency.
14. Thank you, Chief G5 Plans, Col (now Maj-Gen (Ret'd)) Chris Brown, who was a law graduate.

15. Nuclear/Biological/Chemical, now known as Chemical, Biological, Radiological and Nuclear, or CBRN.
16. Otherwise ruefully referred to as a 'wire-brushing'.
17. Or 'ARRCade Confusion' in private.
18. Honestly better than any I have eaten elsewhere, including India.
19. Greece refused to recognize the name Macedonia for this former Yugoslav country, Macedonia itself historically being part of Greece. The country in question was therefore called 'The Former Yugoslav Republic of Macedonia', or FYROM. It formally became The Republic of North Macedonia in 2019, with Greek concurrence.
20. Known as the MUP.
21. *Vojska Jugoslavije*, or VJ.
22. Kosovo Liberation Army, or UCK in Albanian.
23. An émigré in 1948 from Soviet Prague.
24. Supreme Allied Commander Europe, always a US 4* appointment.
25. LOAC – no longer referred to as the law of 'war' to avoid claims that 'we're not bound by it as nobody has declared war', or to put it another way, 'armed conflict' is much easier to define than 'war'.
26. 26 June 1945.
27. Art 1(1).
28. These are in essence economic and/or diplomatic sanctions.
29. The 'P5', decided in 1946 on the basis that they were the world's most powerful nations.
30. If anything, there seemed more likelihood of such an attack by Albania against Serbia, given the declared ambition for a 'Greater Albania'.
31. I ended up running that branch from 2001 for two years and had its name changed to Army Legal Assistance.
32. Maj-Gen Andrew Ridgway.
33. Who took inspiration for some passages in *Lord of the Rings* from his own service on the Somme.
34. Often called Conventions, e.g. the Geneva Conventions 1949.
35. Who, somewhat ironically, resigned from the next Blair government a few years later over the UK's decision to invade Iraq in the second Gulf War.
36. *Opinio juris*. The term 'State practice' refers to general practice by a number of states, not just, for example, repeated practice by a particular state which happens to be an unusually powerful and/or belligerent one.

37. A UNSCR might have worked too, except it could never have passed in that instance because Russia would have vetoed it.
38. It's a bit like Donald Trump saying he has won the election despite the votes; just saying it doesn't make it so, even if you are POTUS.
39. Under the Rome Statute of that year, a treaty which the US has declined to ratify.
40. Former US Secretary of State.
41. A close neighbour to Yugoslavia, religiously as well as geographically.
42. The NAC, NATO's political governing body.
43. Formerly known as Salonika, where somewhat ironically the last time British troops had been deployed was from 1915–18 to defend Serbia from the Central Powers.
44. COMARRC's 'Cabinet' comprising the COS and all staff branch heads, mostly brigadiers with a few lower-ranked add-ons like the LegAd, PolAd (the 'Commissar') and Chief Media Ops.
45. Old Army joke – 'The Army dig in and the RAF check in'.
46. The press did check in there en masse throughout the operation.
47. Just a few miles from Rheindahlen near the Dutch border.
48. He later presented me with a divisional coin, advising me, 'Jim, if you're going to be one, be a Big Red One.' This division was one of the first US divisions deployed to the Western Front in 1917.
49. Particularly timely in their case, as will become clear.
50. Non-alcoholic, sadly – this was the RAF after all.

Chapter 3: The Front-line Factory

1. A grand party hosted for the Duke of Wellington in Brussels on 14/15 June 1815, where he received the news that Napoleon's Grande Armée had crossed the French–Belgian border.
2. On a deployment overseas by invitation the host nation's law will also influence the ROE.
3. Always assuming that the ROE have been competently drafted.
4. In the event that a particular nation has, for example, a political or legal problem with a specific issue like the use of certain weapon systems that nation flags this up on the ROE matrix as a 'national caveat' for commanders to note.
5. Armoured personnel carrier.

Endnotes

6. Although I do recall one phone call with my UK ALS Directorate when I was helpfully informed of arrangements for that summer's annual ALS/RAF Legal Services cricket match! On balance, the absence of 'long screwdriver' interference was not unwelcome.
7. George Bernard Shaw.
8. In 1951.
9. This question proved to be somewhat prophetic because several weeks later, after I had left, a (sober) Scandinavian officer driving a military vehicle though FYROM was involved in a fatal accident and held in local custody for a prolonged period before Richard Batty persuaded the authorities to release him into military jurisdiction.
10. Despite my being confidently assured by a US JAG officer presenting a lecture at Oberammergau that that could never happen.
11. Which they didn't.
12. In fact, Nigel Jones left his comfy desk up in Mons to come and assist.
13. Maybe 750,000.
14. ARRC's Rear Support Command at Thessaloniki actually came under attack from Greek protesters.
15. Op Safe Haven.
16. Which had as its badge a 'Black Adder', irreverently referred to as 'Sammy the Sperm'. The brigade assumed responsibility for setting up the refugee camps in record time, a fantastic achievement.
17. On the night of 27 March, the Serbs shot down an F-117 (supposedly undetectable) Stealth fighter. The pilot bailed out and was rescued by a US heliborne search team from SFOR in Bosnia. A couple of years later I visited the Belgrade air museum where they were proudly selling small patches of the aircraft's top-secret hi-tech 'skin' for €10 apiece – I declined.
18. FYROM had agreed to host NATO land forces preparing to enter Kosovo by invitation, but not as a hostile invader.
19. One morning, when we had been awaiting an order for action from NATO called an 'ACTORD' for several weeks, we learnt that Richard Gere had decided to come and visit the refugees. 'We want an ACTORD, not an ACTOR!' grumbled the COS.
20. Chief PR man was the cockney Jamie Shea who enjoyed daily worldwide airtime for several weeks.
21. I don't think we saw any at all in FYROM.

22. Confidence and Security Building Measures – a political agreement designed to provide full transparency of unusual military concentrations anywhere in Europe.
23. 1977 Geneva Additional Protocol 1 recognizes 'dual use' objects or buildings as legitimate military objectives. NATO maintained the radio station was being used at the time for military purposes.
24. Milosevic was even encouraging the people of Belgrade to stand on the bridges over the Danube at night, defying NATO to bomb them. This presented an interesting legal conundrum as civilians are not lawful targets but they lose protection if directly participating in hostilities. Also, the use of 'human shields' is unlawful.
25. Maybe Slobodan heard I was back!
26. Which SACEUR firmly insisted were *not* 'negotiations'.
27. My wife still has the airmail letter which I wrote her that day, which begins: 'You mustn't throw this letter away because I'm writing it at the conference table at Kumanovo upon which we hope the peace agreement might be signed later today, in which case I might be in Pristina by the time you receive this. It's 12.20 pm and we've been here since about 8.00 pm last night! People laughed at me for bringing my sleeping bag but not anymore.'
28. I was disappointed not to be among them but clearly the legal stuff was all being fed in from London, Washington and Brussels. Interestingly, the 'Commissar', a relatively low-ranked civil servant whose rank had been temporarily inflated, with zero military experience but a hot line to Whitehall, was at the table, yet another clear indication that when push comes to shove politics trumps the law!
29. Russia and probably China would have vetoed it.
30. Greece, for one, would not have allowed it.
31. Although in my view there is a good case for arguing that if an agreement has been secured by dint of seventy-eight days' bombing, the occupation is legally speaking 'belligerent'.
32. Video teleconference.
33. The Stabilization Force, a multinational peacekeeping force based in Sarajevo, Bosnia.
34. See Gen Jackson's autobiography *Soldier* (Bantam 2007).
35. 'Cometh the hour, cometh the man' (John 4:23)

Endnotes

Chapter 4: The Lord Chief Justice of Kosovo

1. AFOR stood for Albania Force, a hastily assembled parallel formation to KFOR deployed in Albania to work with the UCK and help deal with the refugee influx there.
2. Gen Jackson later speculated that he was 'brave as a lion and probably not a bad company commander'.
3. Whom I had last encountered when he was a captain and ADC to the GOC N. Ireland in 1983.
4. The somewhat controversial plan was to reconstitute former KLA fighters as Kosovo police officers.
5. UNSCR 1244 Para 9(d) called upon KFOR to ensure 'public order and safety until the international civil presence can take responsibility for this task'.
6. Camp Bond Steel.
7. They had an extremely efficient 'Staff Judge Advocate' (legal advisor), Major Mark Martins.
8. Status of Mission Agreement, the civilian equivalent of a SOFA, which was being proposed.
9. The Vienna-based Organization for Security and Cooperation in Europe, which had manned the Kosovo Verification Mission from Autumn 1998 until a rapid withdrawal following the Racak killings.
10. Permanent Joint HQ, at Northwood, London, the UK HQ for overseas operations.
11. Led by his laid-back but super-efficient military assistant, Lieutenant Colonel James Everard, who himself recently retired as a four-star general.
12. E.g., the activities of the so called 'Public Interest Law' firm led by the (subsequently struck-off) solicitor Phil Shiner following the second Gulf War.
13. Just a few weeks earlier, on 24 May, Slobodan Milosevic had been indicted by the ICTY on a number of counts including for atrocities allegedly committed on his orders in Kosovo during the preceding months.
14. As previously quoted 'two great nations divided by a common language'.
15. Special Representative of the Secretary-General (of the UN).
16. Tragically killed by a bomb attack on duty for the UN in Baghdad in 2003.
17. In fact, Wellington's army at Waterloo is arguably historically a direct predecessor of the ARRC via its 1(BR) Corps roots.

Chapter 5: ARRC Revisited

1. Son of Gnasher, as *Beano* fans will know.
2. Although it was well known that a regular cargo of suitcases full of misappropriated cash which had been intended for reconstruction of the failed Afghan economy also flew out to Dubai.
3. I never quite got to the bottom of what legal authority the IMP force enjoyed, if any.
4. His career also came to a sticky end, when he was fired by President Obama for unguarded criticisms of the White House reported in a *Rolling Stone* magazine article in 2010.
5. Like a mini-Hercules.

Chapter 6: Welcome to Kabul

1. Of absolutely no significance of course, except perhaps to grandchildren.
2. Called 'Ramzan' locally
3. Short for 'physical training'.
4. During their occupation of Afghanistan, the Russians invariably travelled by road after the Mujahideen learned how to use CIA-supplied Stinger missiles to bring down helicopters. In complete contrast, ISAF reverted to helicopters where possible, as the Taliban had no Stingers but were deadly with IEDs on the roads. They did destroy a Chinook with a lucky RPG shot shortly after I arrived, causing the largest number of US fatalities in one incident of the whole operation, mostly special forces.
5. Reminding me of the character played by Tony Roberts in Woody Allen's 1972 *Play It Again Sam* – I should have told Walt to watch it!
6. The Citadel was the setting for the 1983 film *The Lords of Discipline*, filmed in the UK at my alma mater, Wellington College, a sort of army version of *An Officer and a Gentleman* (1982).
7. CG is the US equivalent of the British GOC (General Officer Commanding). Why would we use two words when three will do? I always used to find it rather demeaning that our general officers wore US rank stars when serving alongside our former colony's generals. It seemed to me that if anything, history should require the opposite.

8. Although by the time I arrived, the latter had been replaced as commander by Gen Allen, also a Marine.
9. From GB in 1919.
10. A military euphemism for a multi-faceted attack involving conventional shooters with vehicles, machine guns and/or RPGs complementing the suicide element.
11. A Farsi word meaning fortified watchtowers.
12. There I met Brig-Gen Mark Martins, last encountered as a major in Kosovo in 1999, who greeted me warmly and took me in hand. He was now the US 'Mr Rule of Law' in Afghanistan but was about to depart to run the commission trying Guantanamo Bay prisoners.
13. Whose inhabitants became known as 'Fobbits'
14. One was supposed to carry a weapon at all times although the requirement also to carry ammunition for it depended on the current threat level. Again, how could this work? It seemed to me all or nothing were the only sensible options. Consequently, unless we were in an 'ammunition to be carried' alert state I would leave both pistol and ammunition in a secure locker in my room.
15. A former subsidiary of Halliburton, run by the one-time US Vice-President Dick Cheney
16. About as much use as bringing their apple-growing expertise to an orange plantation.

Chapter 7: Kill or Capture

1. At least to those who subscribe to the very notion of any law applying, which unfortunately is by no means everybody.
2. Civilian casualty rates: WW1 59%, WW2 67%, Iraq 77%.
3. Fuerzas Armadas Revolucionarias de Colombia, the Revolutionary Armed Forces of Colombia.
4. This tendency led to the adoption by some in ISAF of the label 'fighting aged male' for any male apparently between about 16 and 60, a term whose use was strongly discouraged as reflecting a potentially careless mindset for target identification.
5. Which is itself also a moveable feast under the law.
6. AP1 Art 51(3).
7. Subject to the overriding principle of 'military necessity'.

8. Many of their fighters had no permanent role as insurgents, let alone membership of any proscribed organization, but were hired by the day, before returning to whatever they normally did for a living.
9. The ICRC is acknowledged as the custodian of IHL and has pronounced extensively on this issue.
10. Defined by Interpol as 'money transfer without money movement'.
11. Preparing and having the capacity to attack.
12. The euphemistically named Joint Prioritized Effects List (JPEL).
13. The border following the Durand Line, named after the Victorian British diplomat who established it, was not recognized by the Pashtun anyway.
14. Or even donkeys.
15. AP1 Art. 51.
16. AP1 Art. 57.
17. Even the matter of the ability to continue fighting is not always straightforward, e.g. the Black Knight in *Monty Python and the Holy Grail* (1975), who kept going despite all his limbs being severed: 'it's just a flesh wound'.
18. Compare the Israeli approach to targets in Gaza, a battle space densely inhabited by civilians, causing them great difficulty from tactical to strategic levels.
19. Until that incident Germany had not classified their ISAF deployment as an armed conflict, which they immediately decided to do thereafter to prevent their soldiers potentially facing prosecution by their domestic courts for criminal use of force. This was a first for the country since the Second World War.
20. Their HQ was the 'Quetta Shura', safely tucked away in the Pakistan province of Baluchistan.
21. Perhaps their greatest challenge was to persuade the locals that the law and order offered by central government was as effective as the Taliban's more traditional offering, which tended to be swift, brutal, visible and salutary.
22. There is also a legal obligation to assess new weapons for LOAC compliance, AP1 Art. 36.
23. Mine-Resistant Ambush-Protected Vehicle.
24. The star-studded 1969 satirical WW1 musical epic directed by Richard Attenborough. One of the songs 'Hush, Here Comes a Whizz-bang' sprang to mind.

Endnotes

25. Many Taliban were educated in these schools, which were often Saudi financed.
26. Most had already withdrawn but it had been intended for quite a number to remain behind to help the Iraqi government rebuild the country. The US, understandably, had wanted exclusive criminal jurisdiction over its remaining personnel, which Iraq refused. An example of the potential strategic effect of such 'small print'.
27. A triumph for British military LOAC training – he knew the law (but a pity he chose not to apply it).
28. Even as I write a decade later, atrocities in the form of unlawful killings allegedly committed back then by Australian special forces have just come to light.
29. Ninety-six hours.
30. National Directorate of Security, the Afghan equivalent of the CIA, rumoured to subscribe to somewhat unscrupulous and old-fashioned methods of securing information from the reluctant.
31. The most notorious establishment being Pul-e-Charki prison, Kabul, holding about 5,000 inmates and particularly known for torture and executions during the Soviet occupation.

Chapter 8: Hearts and Minds

1. National Association for Stock Car Auto Racing.
2. An Afghan game like polo played with a goat's carcase instead of a ball.
3. 'Blue on blue' when ISAF killed ISAF or 'blue on green'/'green on blue' if the other party was ANSF.
4. Most famously the Kajaki dam in Helmand, for which hugely expensive hydroelectric turbines were transported across country in a dangerous operation hailed as a military logistic triumph, only to be left to rust, for want of funding or a safe environment to install them.
5. A very frequent and relatively low-risk tactic which was effective in targeting insurgents but highly controversial as they terrified entire villages and inevitably caused innocent casualties.
6. Despite a commander's tactical directive advising otherwise, to avoid upsetting the locals.

Epilogue: *Justitia in Armis*

1. Until recently separate statutes, The Naval Discipline Act 1957, The Army Act 1955 and The Air Force Act 1955, eventually consolidated into the tri-service Armed Forces Act 2006.
2. A classic example of this was the dispute in the Second Gulf War between the UK's force legal adviser in the field and MoD lawyers concerning legal jurisdiction over detainees, a serious dispute in which the former was ultimately vindicated.
3. Visits to the operational theatre can help a lot with this. During my tour I did offer to facilitate a visit by the then Director General, ALS but no joy and as far as I am aware throughout the decade from about 2003 when there were always a number of ALS officers serving with ISAF no Director of ALS paid a visit, although contrastingly, their US JAG 3* counterparts regularly did so.